Picture Processing and Reconstruction

Picture Processing and Reconstruction

Sheldon S. Sandler
Northeastern University

Lexington Books
D.C. Heath and Company
Lexington, Massachusetts
Toronto   London

Library of Congress Cataloging in Publication Data

Sandler, Sheldon Samuel.
 Picture processing and reconstruction.

 Includes index.
 1. Optical data processing. I. Title.
TA1630.S46   621.38'0414   74-25087
ISBN 0-699-97683-0

Published simultaneously in Canada

Printed in the United States of America

International Standard Book Number: 0-669-97683-0

Library of Congress Catalog Card Number: 74-25087

To Barbara and Carolyn

Contents

List of Figures

List of Tables

Preface

Pictures have been with us since caveman times. Artists, not scientists, have shown us how to perceive three-dimensional structure in a two-dimensional painting. The new idea thrust on us by technology is that machines can interpret structure from pictures. Furthermore, technology has given us pictures that are beyond our own physical capabilities of seeing. Surely there is something awe inspiring about taking an X-ray projection picture that is fed directly into a computer which, in turn, produces a real picture for visual interpretation. The reader should be forewarned that the word 'picture' is used throughout this book in a most general sense. Any set of data that can be presented in some type of visual format is considered to be a picture. Indeed, the basic ideas in this book have very broad application to problems in the sciences. The analysis of data for an experiment, for example, could easily correspond to the analysis of a picture representing the data.

This book had its beginning in a course on biological picture processing given at Northeastern University. The original intent of the author was to present a course on reconstruction and picture processing to students from chemistry, biology, and engineering. However, the course was attended nearly exclusively by electrical engineers. The electrical engineering students responded surprisingly well to a wide variety of picture processing techniques that related to the two- and three-dimensional structure of objects. The students as well as the author found the class work and structure problems quite challenging.

This book cannot be regarded as a classic study of the subject. The reader will not find in it, for instance, a predigested summary of articles in the field. Picture processing and reconstruction are presently in a state of rapid change with applications being made in such diverse fields as medicine, geology, molecular biology, astronomy, and electromagnetics. Since the study of picture processing and reconstruction cannot yet be molded into the strictly structured form of the standard textbook, the time for a definitive book lies in the future. The author believes that the present book can serve to introduce the reader to some of the basic ideas involved in using pictures for structural analysis. It is felt, in fact, that the interested reader will be better served at this point by an exposure to new ideas and general concepts with emphasis placed on the need for further development of special techniques for particular applications. The material presented in this book is seen then as a stimulus for future work as well as providing techniques for immediate use.

Acknowledgment

The author acknowledges the help of many people in the preparation of this book. The author's initiation into the subject of reconstruction and picture processing is due to Carolyn Cohen and Donald Caspar, then at Children's Cancer Research Foundation in Boston. The author's sabbatical leave in 1969-70 at the Medical Research Council Laboratory for Molecular Biology, Cambridge, England, was a fruitful year. The guidance and help of Hugh Huxley, Aaron Klug, John Finch, Tony Crowther, and Linda Amos are gratefully acknowledged. The National Science Foundation's support for the author (under Grant GB-30320 with Northeastern University) was instrumental in helping him to carry out the basic work relating to picture processing. Professor Harold Raemer, Chairman of the Department of Electrical Engineering at Northeastern University, was instrumental in providing the time and encouragement to undertake this book. Thanks are also due Mrs. M. Schnabel for typing most of the final draft of the manuscript and Ms. Margaret Owens for correcting the original manuscript and proofreading the galley proofs. Finally the author gratefully acknowledges the help and assistance given by the students in the course Biological Picture Processing.

Picture Processing and Reconstruction

1 Introduction

A picture consists of light and dark segments that are presented in a one-, two-, or three-dimensional image. It is no surprise that engineers and scientists are constantly faced with interpreting and understanding such images. The surprise is that there are many pictures that require more than a simple visual interpretation. Furthermore, there are cases where the amount of pictorial information is so large that machine assistance is required. The main purpose of this book is to help the reader to interpret pictures to obtain structural information. This interpretation will require a basic understanding of picture processing. Machine and optical methods will be required to operate on the pictures. These methods serve to transform the pictures into other pictures that are more easily interpreted by the eye.

The variety of pictures is so immense that no book of this size could cover them all. The nature of picture processing for structural information is such that both specific and ad hoc methods can be used. Both approaches will be covered. The basic ideas presented here are meant not only for direct application but also to encourage the reader to develop special methods for particular applications. Some important problem areas are presented in this chapter. They deal mainly with pictures that are produced by signals that travel through objects. The pictorial result of these signals is a superposition of depth effects. The simplest case consists of a one-dimensional scan that is compressed into a point of information. Obvious extensions lead to lines, and to planes.

Three specific examples are given in this chapter that involve some type of picture as an output. The examples are all concerned with processes that produce a projection picture. The examples are not meant to be complete, but rather to familiarize the reader with the relation between a physical process and its corresponding picture. The properties of projection or transmission pictures are described in Chapter 2. The first example concerns X-ray astronomy in space, the second, geophysical exploration, and the last, biological pictures. The first example briefly describes the physical background needed to understand the meaning of the light and dark segments of a solar X-ray picture. The solar X-ray pictures have recently (1975) been used to generate three-dimensional representations of some solar features. The reconstruction methods of Chapter 4 have been found applicable to this case. The second example shows the processes that produce a picture for locating objects or interfaces in the earth. The problem of interpreting these pictures for structural information is more involved than in the first example due to the multidimensional nature of the probing signal. The last example is involved mainly with pictures taken on an electron microscope (EM). The projection pictures here contain information that is usually "buried," to use an engineering term, in the noise. Special techniques, such as optical diffraction, could make the geometric properties of the picture more apparent to the viewer. These techniques are described in Chapter 3. Reconstruction methods described in Chapter 3 for Fourier space and in Chapter 4 for real space are applicable to biological pictures.

Solar X-Ray Astronomy

An area of potential application of three-dimensional reconstruction techniques is in the observation of the structure of emission features in the sun's outer atmosphere, the solar corona.[a] The corona consists of a highly ionized plasma at temperatures in excess of one million degrees Kelvin. The characteristic emission from such a plasma is in the soft X-ray region of the electromagnetic spectrum (1-60 Å in wavelength).

Emission from the corona may therefore be studied without interference from background photospheric and chromospheric radiation. The coronal plasma is very diffuse, and optically thin (i.e., X-rays are not significantly absorbed in the corona). However, observations of the X-ray corona must be made from rockets or satellites in order to overcome the problem of absorption in the earth's atmosphere. More detailed description of the X-ray corona may be found in Vaiana, et al. [7, 9].

The development of an instrument capable of observing coronal X-rays with sufficient spatial, spectral, and temporal resolution to provide significant information concerning coronal structure and dynamics has been a formidable task. It has required the design, fabrication, and calibration of unconventional optics for the soft X-ray region along with the choice of a suitable detector (photographic film) and the selection of pass bands for the broad-band filters and dispersive elements.

These difficulties have been overcome with the development at American Science and Engineering of grazing incidence reflecting telescopes. A picture and a schematic diagram of the AS & E telescope flown as a part of the Apollo Telescope Mount on the Skylab Earth orbiting laboratory are shown in Figures 1-1 and 1-2. The X-ray image is formed by the grazing incidence reflection from confocal and coaxial paraboloidal and hyperboloidal surfaces. This combination permits the focusing of incident parallel radiation over a large field of view with relatively short focal length by a

---

[a]This section was prepared by Drs. J.T. Nolte, and J.K. Silk, American Science and Engineering, Cambridge, Massachusetts. This work was supported by NASA, Marshall Space Flight Center, under contract NAS 8-27758.

Courtesy of A. Krieger, American Science and Engineering.

Figure 1-1. X-Ray Telescope

single reflection from each surface. The Skylab instrument makes use of a nested pair of telescopes for greater collecting area. A filter wheel and an objective grating spectrometer permit observations in different wavelength ranges, thus providing information on the X-ray spectrum. Details of the design of the instrument are discussed by Vaiana, et al. [8]. The development of the grazing incidence telescope, and a brief comparison with other methods of X-ray photography may be found in Vaiana, et al. [9].

A sample X-ray image taken by the AS & E instrument on Skylab is shown in Figure 1-3. The spatial resolution is about 2 arc seconds (1400 km). The coronal structures are studied by the analysis of many images such as this.

The analysis begins with the determination of the energy deposited on

4

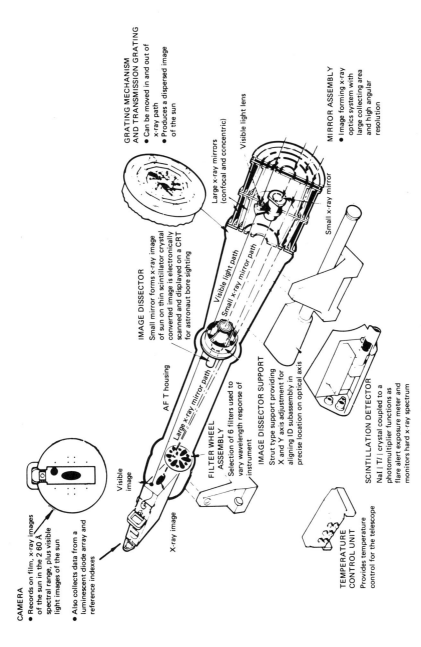

CAMERA
- Records on film, x-ray images of the sun in the 2 60 Å spectral range, plus visible light images of the sun
- Also collects data from a luminescent diode array and reference indexes

Visible image

X-ray image

IMAGE DISSECTOR
Small mirror forms x-ray image of sun on thin scintillator crystal converted image is electronically scanned and displayed on a CRT for astronaut bore sighting

A F T housing

Visible light path

Small x-ray mirror path

Large x-ray mirror path

FILTER WHEEL ASSEMBLY
Selection of 6 filters used to vary wavelength response of instrument

IMAGE DISSECTOR SUPPORT
Strut type support providing X and Y axis adjustment for aligning ID subassembly in precise location on optical axis

GRATING MECHANISM AND TRANSMISSION GRATING
- Can be moved in and out of x-ray path
- Produces a dispersed image of the sun

Large x-ray mirrors (confocal and concentric)

Visible light lens

Small x-ray mirror

MIRROR ASSEMBLY
- Image forming x-ray optics system with large collecting area and high angular resolution

SCINTILLATION DETECTOR
NaI | Tℓ| crystal coupled to a photomultiplier functions as flare alert exposure meter and monitors hard x-ray spectrum

TEMPERATURE CONTROL UNIT
Provides temperature control for the telescope

Figure 1-2. Schematic Diagram of AS & E X-Ray Telescope

Courtesy of A. Krieger, American Science and Engineering.

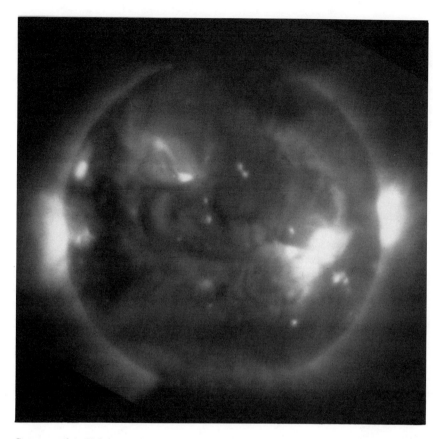

Courtesy of A. Krieger, American Science and Engineering.

Figure 1-3. Sample X-Ray Image of the Sun, Taken by AS & E Instrument on Skylab

the film from the photographic density in the image measured with a microdensitometer. This is done using the results of film calibration measurements such as reported by Vaiana, et al. [8]. The energy per unit area deposited on the film through a particular filter I_{filt} is related to the emission from a coronal feature ρ by

$$I_{\text{filt}}(x, y) = Kt \int_0^\infty dl \int_{x'_1}^{x'_2} dx' \int_{y'_1}^{y'_2} dy' \int_{\lambda_1}^{\lambda_2} d\lambda$$

$$\times \ N_e^2(x', y', l) \, n_{\text{filt}}(x', y', x, y, \lambda) \rho(x', y', \lambda, T(x', y', l))$$

where $\qquad K = $ constant

$\qquad\qquad t = $ exposure time

x', y' and l are the coordinates of the emitting region, with l the distance along the line of sight

N_e = electron density

n_{filt} = filter transmission times the telescope response (point spread function)

ρ = power emitted at wavelength λ by unit emission measure at temperature T

The integrals over x', y' and l include the entire field of view of the telescope; the integral over λ includes all contributing wavelengths. The point spread response function is involved in determining the resolution of the telescope. Samples of the point spread function for two different wavelengths for a point source of radiation on the optical axis of the telescope ($x' = y' = 0$) are given in Vaiana, et al. [8]. In general, the point spread function depends on both the wavelength and the location of the source relative to the optical axis of the instrument (i.e., a point source near the edge of the field of view does not have a symmetric image). The dependence of ρ on x', y' can be found from the measured $I_{filt}(x, y)$ by a deconvolution procedure, using the measured point spread function. The deconvolved image obtained in this way may be interpreted as a projection image of the emission structure of the solar corona. Since the sun rotates (at a rate of approximately 13.2 degrees per day), images taken at different times are different views of the coronal structure. These views may be used to attempt a reconstruction of the three-dimensional structure.

There are two special problems involved in reconstructing the coronal emission structure. The first of these is that the sun's axis of rotation may be as much as 7 degrees away from perpendicular to the line of sight. This problem may be overcome by an appropriate generalization of methods that assume rotation perpendicular to the viewing direction. The second problem is the temporal evolution of the corona during the time required for rotation through an angle large enough to permit reconstruction. This difficulty may be circumvented by using a small angular spread, or by averaging to remove changes (either of which implies coarser resolution of the structure) or by choosing only those structures that can be shown to remain stable on a time scale of several days.

Transmission Pictures in Geophysical Exploration

The following section is concerned with the exploration of the subsurface of the earth. An experiment is described that tries to determine if buried ice can be located in a permanently frozen region, called permafrost. Sensors and sounders are available to explore the earth over the entire electromagnetic spectrum. Acoustic sounders have been generally used for geophysical exploration. An acoustic sounder is usually used to produce a burst of low frequency waves. The waves travel with a velocity that is a function of the physical properties of the earth. When the waves meet a section of earth with different physical properties, a portion of the wave is reflected back to a sensor. Sometimes the source and sounder are located in different positions. In this case a one-way propagation path is involved in the search; otherwise a two-way path is relevant. As an example, consider the case of a source and sensor at the same location. A sensor record would show a number of reflected pulses that correspond to different layers in the earth. The time scale on the record can be converted into a distance scale once the velocity of propagation through the entire material is known.

The electromagnetic sounder described in the following section is similar to the acoustic sounder already described. However the electromagnetic source here is an unmodulated, extremely short-duration pulse. The scanning is along the earth with the sounder and sensor in the same location. The two-dimensional plots, or pictures, are obtained by superimposing discrete pulse reflection records. The discrete records correspond to different horizontal positions along the surface of the earth.

The Distribution of Ground Ice in Permafrost

It is important to know the distribution of both permafrost and ground ice in the arctic and subarctic regions. This importance is associated with construction and land use in these areas. An experiment described by Campbell and Sandler [1] was designed to see if electromagnetic subsurface profiling (ESP) can locate masses of ground ice in permafrost. The ESP method provides a continuous record of subsurface soil conditions to a depth of 25 feet. This profile or record is usually presented as a two-dimensional picture.

Description of the Problem. A thorough understanding of permafrost is essential to the successful development or use of many arctic and subarctic areas. Most of the land area of North America above 52° north latitude is underlaid by either continuous or discontinuous permafrost. In general, areas of continuous permafrost are characterized by permafrost of continuous lateral extent, except in areas covered by large bodies of water. Areas of discontinuous permafrost are characterized by large areas of unfrozen ground between irregular bodies of permafrost. The thickness of permafrost varies considerably, but is known, according to Ferrians [3], to be at least as much as 1330 feet in some areas.

Structural and compositional relationships within permafrost and between permafrost and the surrounding unfrozen soil may be complex. Figure 1-4 shows the distribution of permafrost in North America. The following basic types of permafrost have been defined by Sterns [6]:

1. *Frozen soils in which segregated ice is not obvious.* This condition exists when the amount of moisture is so low that very little ice is present and the soil or rock is dry frozen and may be friable. It also exists at moderate to high degrees of saturation with ice films or tiny crystals cementing the soil into a hard, solid mass. The amount of ice may range from zero to a volume in excess of the volume of voids.

2. *Frozen soils with visible segregated ice in amount secondary to the volume of soil.* The ice may appear as visible crystals of about the same size as the soil particles, as ice coatings over soil particles, or as small lenses, veins, or visible frost.

3. *Frozen soils with larger concentrations of ice (greater than 1 inch) within the soil mass.* The inclusions may be lenses, layers, veins, wedges, sheets, or similar formations. These substantial ice strata or bodies are designated as segregated ice, but are less extensive than the ground ice masses 4 and 5.

4. *Massive ice with soil inclusions.* This is predominantly ice with a small portion of its volume in the form of concentrated soil inclusions such as pockets, streaks, discoloration, and thin layers. Frozen ground of types 2 and 3 gives the appearance of soil even though it may contain as much as 80% ice by volume. Massive ice appears as solid ice, clear, milky, discolored, or frosty with air bubbles.

5. *Ice without soil inclusions.* Clear massive ice many feet thick may be present under a surface layer of vegetation and soil. It may be folded and distorted or unaltered.

6. The term "relict ice" has been used for large masses of buried ice presumed to have broken off a retreating ice cap and been subsequently covered by glacial outwash.

In many cases, subsurface investigation is necessary to determine which type(s) of permafrost, if any, lies under a particular area. It is generally agreed that a complete knowledge and understanding of subsurface conditions are requisite to the successful construction of buildings, roads, dams, pipelines, and other man-made structures. This is particularly true in areas underlaid by permafrost. If the extent and character of permafrost are not taken into consideration during the design of man-made structures, the thermal equilibrium between permafrost and its surroundings may be upset during construction or subsequent use. Significant ground subsidence could result, leading to costly repairs or abandonment of a particular structure. Conventional methods of subsurface exploration in permafrost

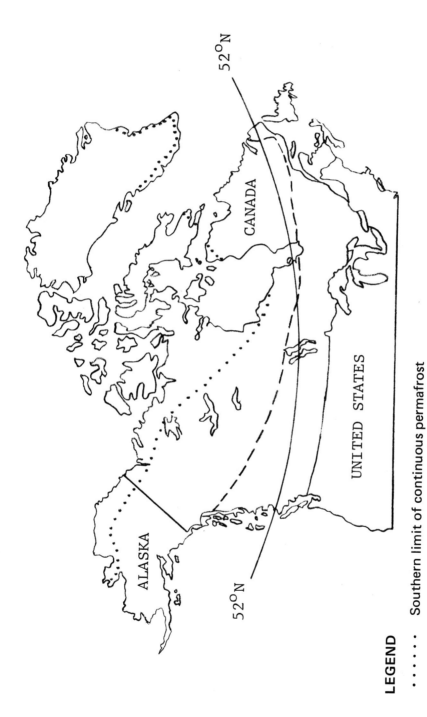

Figure 1-4. Distribution of Permafrost in North America

CANADA

UNITED STATES

52°N

ALASKA

LEGEND

· · · · · · Southern limit of continuous permafrost

― ― ― Southern limit of discontinuous permafrost

areas have been used with limited success. Borings have been used in many areas, but they generally give an incomplete, and often misleading, picture of subsurface conditions. Seismic and other geophysical methods have been used with less success. The complex internal structure and irregular upper surface of permafrost require that an accurate, continuous profile of subsurface conditions be available to the designer of any structure. Electromagnetic Subsurface Profiling (ESP) can provide this information, particularly in areas where large masses of ground ice, including ice wedges, are present in the permafrost.

Description of the ESP System. Basically, the ESP System is the electromagnetic equivalent of the seismic method of geophysical exploration. The waves produced by the seismic sounder are known to propagate in a wide variety of materials. Since the seismic pulses are localized in time, it is possible to differentiate soil and rock strata by separating the received pulses on a time scale. The seismic pulse may be conceptualized as a burst of energy that is modified in velocity and shape as it progresses through the earth. The electromagnetic equivalent of the longitudinal acoustic waves used in seismic sounders is the transverse electromagnetic wave. These waves are produced electrically by discharging a battery into a special wave launching device. The duration of these discharges is on the order of one nanosecond (10^{-9} seconds). A fast switch is used to create a time-limited signal which is sent directly to the wave launching device during the transmit cycle. The transmitted wave is reflected from the various soil and rock strata in the earth. The reflection phenomenon will be discussed later. The reflected signal is picked up by the same device used for launching the transmitted wave. A selector then channels the returned signal to a receiving device. The received signal is usually stored on magnetic tape to facilitate high speed mapping and further processing. A block diagram of the system is shown in Figure 1-5. A signal recorded in practice is shown in Figure 1-6. The earth's surface is shown on the top line, and depth into the earth is in the downward direction. The "profile" has been produced by printing high signal levels as black and no signal as white. Intermediate signals are in the gray range.

Return now to the question of what physical principles are involved in producing reflections from soil and rock strata. This question is difficult to answer directly if the exploration is given in the "real" domain of time. A time-domain analysis is available but awkward to use, and it is difficult to give simple explanations for the phenomena. Another procedure is more useful, both in the analysis and in providing a result that is readily interpreted in a physical way. The basis of the analysis is the fact that time-limited signals can be represented by a superposition of harmonic or steady-state solutions. Each steady-state solution has a complex amplitude

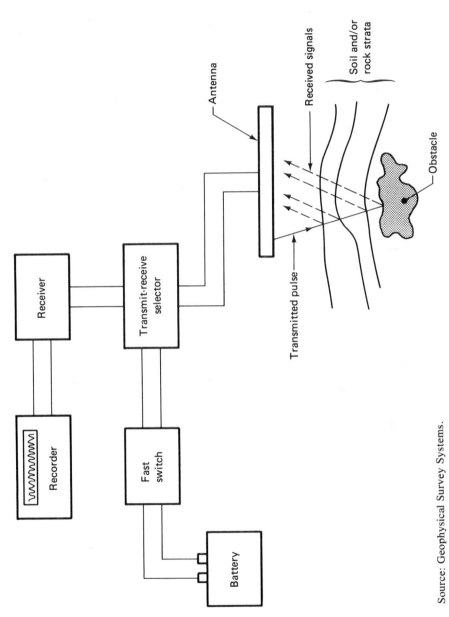

Source: Geophysical Survey Systems.

Figure 1-5. Block Diagram of ESP System

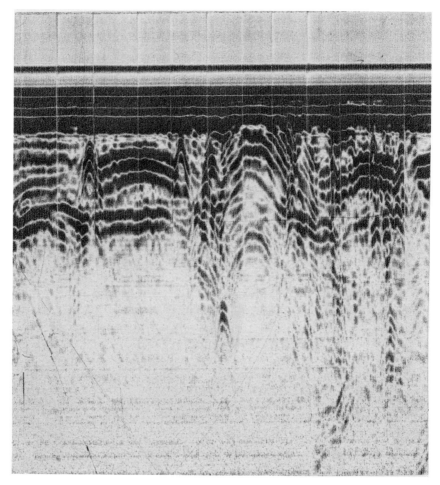

Courtesy of Geophysical Survey Systems.

Figure 1-6. A Sample ESP Printout

associated with it. The steady-state analysis provides a way of determining the final complex amplitudes after the waves have been reflected by a layer of material. A superposition of the reflected waves yields the time-domain reflected pulse. It should be noted that the superposition is equivalent to an integration procedure. This integration procedure involves the Fourier transformation of the time-domain function. A forward transformation is used to go from the time domain to the frequency domain and an inverse transformation is used to return to the time domain.

The time-limited signal shown in Figure 1-7 is assumed to be Gaussian in

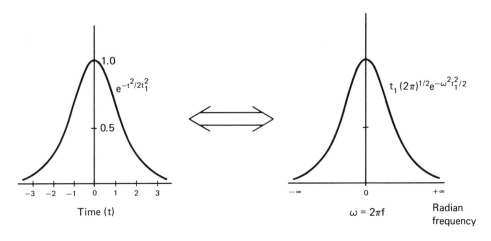

Figure 1-7. Fourier Spectrum of a Time-limited Signal (Gaussian)

form. Actually, this is close to the form it has in practice since there is a finite rise and decay time. The Gaussian pulse $f(t)$ is represented mathematically by the relation

$$f(t) = e^{-t^2/2t_1^2} \tag{1.1}$$

where t_1 determines the width of the pulse. The pulse given by 1.1 can be decomposed into a frequency spectrum $F(\omega)$ where

$$F(\omega) = \int_{-\infty}^{\infty} f(t) e^{j\omega t} \, dt \tag{1.2}$$

If $f(t)$ is given by 1.1, then the corresponding spectrum $F(\omega)$ can be found from 1.2, or

$$F(\omega) = t_1 (2\pi)^{1/2} e^{-\omega^2 t_1^2/2} \tag{1.3}$$

From equation 1.3 it can be shown that a narrow temporal pulse is associated with a wide frequency spectrum. For example, if the time pulse is the order of one nanosecond in half width, then the frequency spectrum extends from zero to about 350 MHz. The response $R(\omega)$ of the earth to a harmonic signal can be calculated for a single frequency. The actual reflected signal in the time domain is then obtained by superposition. Thus the time response $r(t)$ that corresponds to $R(\omega)$ is

$$r(t) = \frac{1}{2\pi} \int_{-\infty}^{\infty} R(\omega) F(\omega) e^{-j\omega t} \, d\omega \tag{1.4}$$

where $F(\omega)$ is the pulse spectrum. The relevant quantity for earth exploration is the reflection coefficient R. For a two layered medium it is

$$R = \frac{k_2 - k_1}{k_2 + k_1} \tag{1.5}$$

$$\left.\begin{array}{l} k_1^2 = \omega^2\mu_1\epsilon_1 - j\omega\mu_1\sigma_1 \\ k_2^2 = \omega^2\mu_2\epsilon_2 - j\omega\mu_2\sigma_2 \end{array}\right\} \tag{1.6}$$

where μ = magnetic constant

        ϵ = electric (or dielectric) constant

        σ = conductivity

Equation 1.5 shows that an electromagnetic signal (at a single frequency ω) gives rise to a reflected signal that is proportional to the difference in the electrical properties of the materials. Since the propagation factors given by 1.6 are frequency dependent, it appears possible to find some frequencies that give rise to large reflections, and others for which there is a negligible returned signal. The ESP System takes advantage of this relation in producing an extremely wide-band pulse from which it is usually possible to produce an appreciable reflection.

Consider the simple example shown in Figure 1-8. A half plane of firn, ice, or frozen ground is irradiated with a normally incident electric field E_i. The reflected field is E_r. The time history of the reflected signal is shown for the three different materials. Note that the amplitude of the three signals has an appreciable difference near the maximum value of reflected field. This difference would appear as a different level of gray in a black-white picture.

The depth of penetration of the signal is not only dependent on the strength of the signal; it is also dependent on the frequency content of the pulse. For example, the properties of the earth generally allow the low-frequency component to propagate. It is, however, the higher frequency components that give rise to resolution. The present system has the capability of using short pulses for near surface work (i.e., larger high-frequency content) and wider pulses for deep penetration.

In an attempt to simulate ground ice, six tons of block ice were buried in interbedded sand and silt. An ice "lens" and an ice "wedge" were constructed. A hole in which no ice was buried was excavated and backfilled to show the effects on ESP data of backfilling alone. A plan view of the "lens," "wedge," and backfilled hole are shown in Figure 1-9. A cross section of the "lens" and "wedge" in place is shown in Figure 1-10. Photos of the "wedge" during and after construction are shown in Figures 1-11 and 1-12. ESP scans were taken before and after the ice "lens" and ice "wedge" were constructed. The location of the scans and the direction in which each scan was taken is shown in Figure 1-9. Results of each scan are

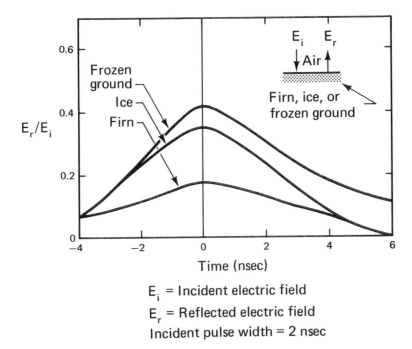

Source: Geophysical Survey Systems.

Figure 1-8. Reflected Signal from Firn, Ice, and Frozen Ground for a Gaussian Incident Pulse (Theoretical)

shown graphically as an ESP printout in Figures 1-13 through 1-17. Each printout represents a continuous "profile" (geologic section) in the vertical plane, showing subsurface soil and soil-ice interfaces to depths of as much as 13 feet. The "lens" and "wedge" are clearly shown on the printouts, but the presence of the backfilled hole is not as obvious. It should be apparent from these examples that skilled geologic interpretation of ESP data will be required to locate accurately large masses of ground ice in their natural environment.

Biological Pictures

Many obstacles prevent the physical and biological scientist from meeting on some common ground. The rapid advance of science in the twentieth century has brought with it an increased specialization of individual disciplines. Thus, separate modes of communication have evolved that have

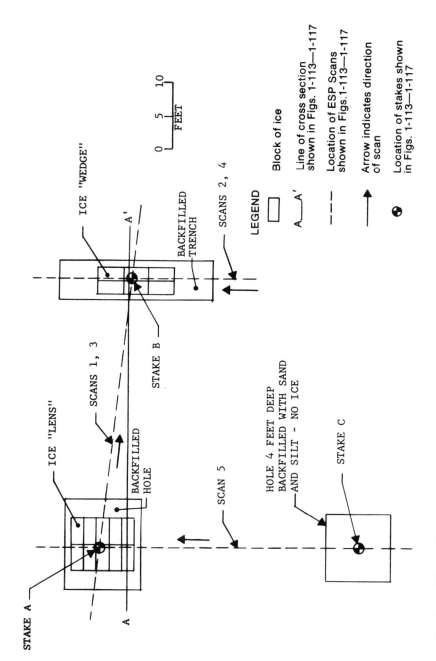

Source: Geophysical Survey Systems.

Figure 1-9. Plan View of Ice ''Lens,'' Ice ''Wedge,'' and Backfilled Hole with No Ice

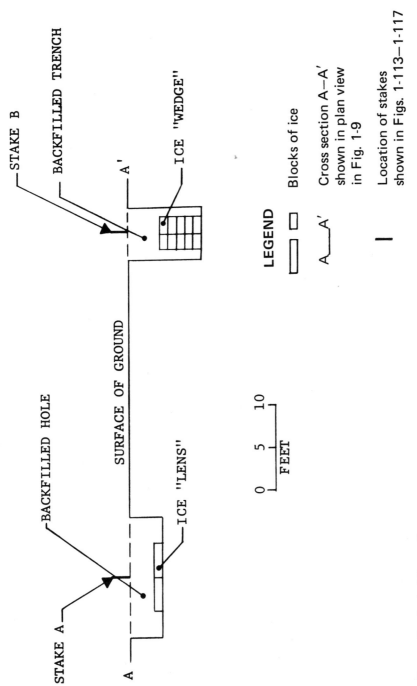

Figure 1-10. Cross Section of Ice "Lens" and Ice "Wedge"

Source: Geophysical Survey Systems.

Courtesy of Geophysical Survey Systems.

Figure 1-11. Ice "Wedge" under Construction

served to exclude outsiders. The major difficulties are not only semantic, but also philosophical and didactical. What have evolved between the physical scientist and the biologist are fundamentally different methods of approach and thinking patterns. Some oversimplified descriptions will serve to illustrate the vast gulf between the two. The physical scientist is continually faced with a variety of very structured problems. These problems are reduced through physical laws to a formalism. The formalism in turn is expressed by a mathematical description and solved in mathematical terms. The biologist is much more verbal in the sense that he is able to

Courtesy of Geophysical Survey Systems.

Figure 1-12. Completed Ice "Wedge"

express complicated interrelations between biological forms in non-mathematical terms. The verbal description is underlaid by a very sophisticated methodology that is not apparent to the physical scientist. Further differences between the two are found in their statements of what constitutes the problems and the solutions. The problems faced by the physical scientist can usually be stated in very precise terms. The biologist may spend a major part of his time trying to find what questions to ask. The answer may turn out to be a fact, an interrelation, or a pictorial description.

One common tool used by biologists and physical scientists is the biological picture. The goal is to produce a two- or three-dimensional representation of a biological object or system. The picture is then the medium of communication available to the biologist and understood by the physical scientist. This approach says that the biological "answer," if any is possible, is a structure or form. The interpretation of the form is left to the beholder. All that is said here is that the picture is an important piece of evidence. The production of the least biased and most meaningful picture is the major part of the task that is presented.

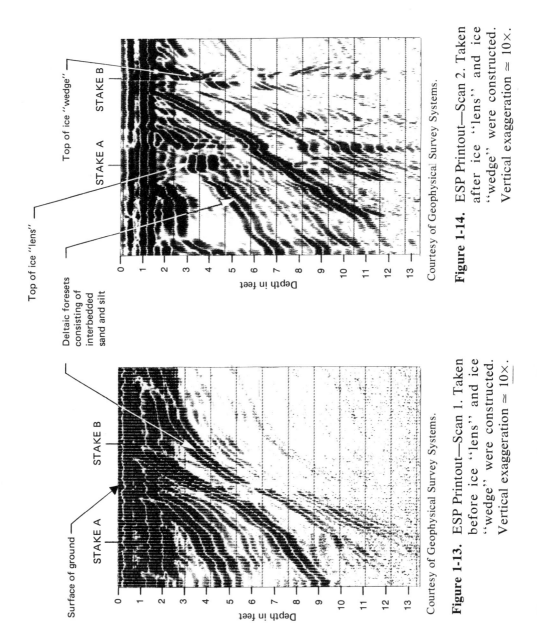

Courtesy of Geophysical Survey Systems.

Figure 1-14. ESP Printout—Scan 2. Taken after ice "lens" and ice "wedge" were constructed. Vertical exaggeration ≅ 10×.

Courtesy of Geophysical Survey Systems.

Figure 1-13. ESP Printout—Scan 1. Taken before ice "lens" and ice "wedge" were constructed. Vertical exaggeration ≅ 10×.

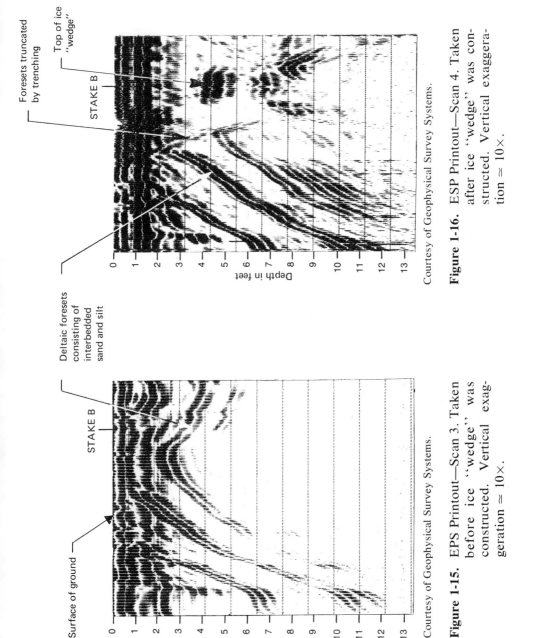

Courtesy of Geophysical Survey Systems.

Figure 1-16. ESP Printout—Scan 4. Taken after ice "wedge" was constructed. Vertical exaggeration ≈ 10×.

Courtesy of Geophysical Survey Systems.

Figure 1-15. EPS Printout—Scan 3. Taken before ice "wedge" was constructed. Vertical exaggeration ≈ 10×.

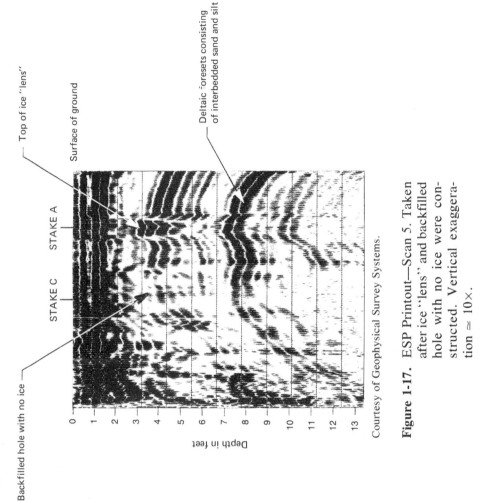

Courtesy of Geophysical Survey Systems.

Figure 1-17. ESP Printout—Scan 5. Taken after ice "lens" and backfilled hole with no ice were constructed. Vertical exaggeration ≈ 10×.

The production of a pictorial representation would be a great deal easier if the human eye were a precision instrument. That the eye is, however, far from an objective observer is well documented in the literature [4]. The eye, for example, likes to group large amounts of information into smaller groups. Consider the array of dots shown in Figure 1-18. The eye in scanning the picture continually regroups the array in rows or columns, or smaller subsets. The eye also has the unfortunate habit of continually trying to make order out of disorder. Figure 1-19 shows an array of dots that are not aligned on any particular lattice. However, the eye in looking at the picture tries to pick out discrete sections to place them in a preconceived order (e.g., rectangular, hexagonal, or triangular). The eye also likes to interpret an object in terms of its background. The arrow illusion of Figure 1-20 shows two lines of identical length, with arrows pointing inward or outward. The eye interprets the line with inward arrows as shorter than that with outward arrows.

The previous examples help explain the problems in using the unaided eye as a research tool. This is not to say that visual intuition is not an aid in pictorially representing an object. Rather it is desirable to use whatever tools available to generate more unbiased optical and mathematical methods for picture processing. Furthermore, most biological pictures contain more information than can be assimilated by the naked eye. This information can be gathered by processing the picture optically in some way. This processing reduces the visual complexity of the picture to a more easily assimilated form.

Some biological pictures are quite foreign to the eye. For example, under ordinary conditions, objects are perceived by scattered light. Objects are recognized mostly by their surface shapes. Seldom is the eye required to "scan" the volume of an object in order to recognize it. This leads us to a major example of a biological picture that the eye is not prepared to interpret. This type of picture is called a transmission picture. It is made by shining light or sending an electron beam through an object and recording the "shadow" image on a photographic plate. This situation is represented graphically in Figure 1-21. A parallel light source to the left illuminates an object. The object here consists of a gel in which three opaque cylinders are placed parallel to the faces of the section. The shadow picture is shown on the right. Note that the height of the shadow from each of the three cylinders is the same. Evidently, there is no way of telling from the picture the specific location of the objects in the original cross section. This is the basic problem posed by the reconstruction of an object. The answer lies in precisely locating the distribution of matter in the test section.

There are many cases of interest, including the practically important one of using the electron microscope where it is not possible to gain

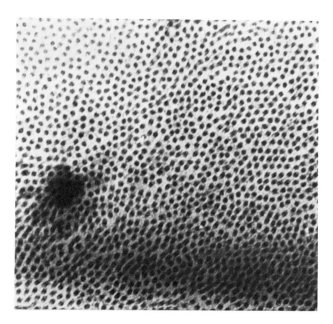

Electron micrograph by the author.

Figure 1-18. A Posterior Section of the Human Cornea

sufficient data for reconstruction from available transmission pictures. Two possible alternatives are either to make sufficient assumptions about the original object to effect a reconstruction, or to work with the data in a nondeterministic way. Sometimes it is not even possible to consider a reconstruction in the usual sense. Still, it may be possible through indirect optical methods to say something about the order within the object or the important geometrical distances without localizing either the order or the distances.

Superficially one might consider the reconstruction process as just another problem in pattern recognition. As is practically evident, however, pattern recognition has not been successful in an ad hoc way. Each physical recognition problem has its own peculiarities. The nature of the recognition depends on all the processes that are involved in making the picture. Only with an understanding of the nature of biological-specimen preparation and of the available optical and electron optical devices can an understanding of the biological picture be possible. Biological pictures, to mention one difficulty, are generally not pleasing to the eye. They contain a great deal of noise (i.e., dirt), which sometimes makes it difficult to distinguish the desired object from its background. Some of the noise or clutter is due to

Figure 1-19. An Array of Dots

the specimen-preparation processes, while some is due to the optical process that was used to produce the picture.

A general word to the reader on the practical problems of specimen preparation for picture production is in order. Biological objects generally must be "coaxed" into getting their picture taken. Some of the best pictures (which actually happen to be X-rays) are taken by first coaxing the biological object into forming a crystal that has some structural stability.

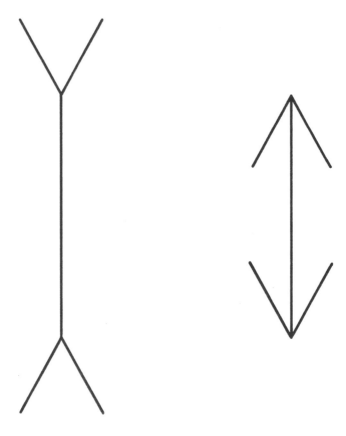

Figure 1-20. The Muller-Lyer or Arrow Illusion

Microscope and electron microscope pictures, on the other hand, involve a lot of dissecting, cutting, chemical treatment, and staining before a picture may be taken. This is the nature of the art, and is something that one must live with. Before treatment, the objects were "wiggly" and transparent. After treatment, the objects have some structural stability and sufficient contrast to be seen.

Microscopy and Specimen Preparation

A large variety of optical and electron optical instruments are available for biological-specimen investigation. For a discussion of some of these, see Cosslett [2] or Slayter [5]. The gross structure can be viewed with a magnifying glass having a magnification of the order of 20×. Specimens in

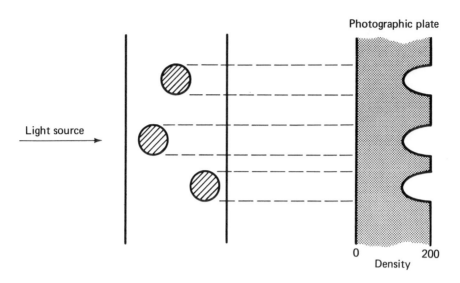

Figure 1-21. Opaque Objects Illuminated by a Light Source

the range from 10 to 1000 microns (micron $\mu = 10^{-6}$m) can be viewed in a compound microscope. From 1μ through to the Angstrom ($\text{Å} = 10^{-10}$m = $10^4\mu$) range, the electron microscope (designated EM) serves as the most commonly used optical viewer. The large useful range of the electron microscope allows one to view bacteria, viruses, micromolecules, molecules, and even atoms. A diagram of an electron microscope is shown in Figure 1-22. The cathode consists of a hairpin filament centered on a hole in a circular bias shield. The accelerating voltage is of the order of 100 kv, although much higher values are also in use. A series of magnetic lenses is used to focus and control the electron beam. The entire structure is operated in a high vacuum. As a consequence, specimens that are inserted into the column become dehydrated. The electrons actually pass through the specimen and are viewed on a fluorescent screen located at the base of the column. A permanent record is made of the image by swinging away the fluorescent screen and allowing the electron beam to strike a glass photographic plate.

The wavelength of the illumination should be appreciably smaller than the characteristic lengths associated with the object being viewed. The wavelength λ of yellow light is about 5000 Å. This limits the use of optical microscopes to objects above the micron range. The electron microscope, however, has an effective wavelength that is inversely proportional to the square root of the accelerating voltage. An approximate relation given by Slayter is

$$\lambda = 12.27/\sqrt{V} \text{ (Å)} \qquad (1.7)$$

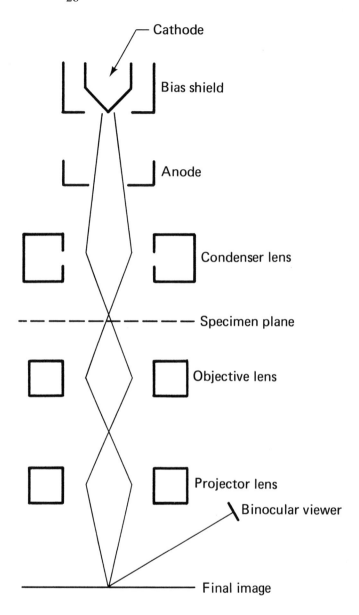

Figure 1-22. Electron Microscope

The relation 1.7 states that for an acceleration voltage of 100 kv the effective wavelength is 0.037 Å. The limit of resolution in an electron microscope is not determined by the accelerating voltage, but rather is due to the optical defects in the focusing systems and to the basic mechanical problems encountered in the construction of such a precision instrument.

There is a basic difference between the methods of achieving contrast in the optical and electron microscopes. In both types of instruments, sufficient contrast for viewing must be obtained by treating the specimen chemically. In the optical microscope, however, the light through the specimen is changed in amplitude and phase, while in the EM the contrast is due to differential scattering. This effect is based on the fact that the scattering of electrons from the positive nucleus of an atom is proportional to the atomic number of the material. The electrons in the microscope beam are scattered from the heavy atoms that have been dispersed throughout the volume of the material. Positive staining, for example, consists of treating the sections of the specimen with solutions of the salts of heavy metals. Parts of the specimen where the staining is light are less affected by the beam than those in the dense area. The difference in the scattering between the areas of different density produces the contrast.

The preparation of sections for electron microscopy is a significant technical achievement. The section thicknesses range from 150 Å to about 700 Å and require very specialized instruments. Since specimen preparation has much to do with picture effects, it is well briefly to review the methods of producing a biological section for the EM.

The biological specimen used for EM investigation is first reduced to sufficiently small pieces so that the subsequent chemical treatment will act uniformly throughout the volume. Pieces of the order of a few millimeters in length are required. If the specimens are already less than this in length, so much the better. The type of treatment described here is used for obtaining a direct transmission picture. If the object is too large for a direct transmission picture, other techniques are available. For example, a replica or cast could be made from the specimen, then treated and examined in the electron microscope.

The specimen pieces are first reduced to a neutral pH of 7 by buffering and testing with a pH meter. The pieces are then dehydrated by replacing the water with alcohol or acetone. Gradually increasing percentages of alcohol or acetone are added to the mixture until all the water in the specimen has been replaced.

One of the major accomplishments is the achievement of enough contrast in the specimen to be seen in the electron microscope. A fixative, usually gluteraldehyde, is added to the dehydrated specimen. Such fixatives are very successful in increasing the contrast between proteins and their surrounding structure. There is usually a specific fixative and stain for a particular biological material. A strong oxidation agent, osmium tetroxide, is used to effect an increase in contrast by selective oxidation of the different parts of the specimen. The specimen is then ready to be imbedded in plastic so that it may be cut into thin slices. The plastic, usually aradite or epon, is added to the mixture in liquid form. Hardening is achieved with additives and an acceleration agent. The specimen imbedded in the plastic mixture can be oven hardened in a vertical mold. The resulting capsule shape is called a block. Sometimes it is more convenient to pour the specimen and plastic mixture into a flat dish. The hardened result can be cut out with a thin saw and mounted at the end of a previously prepared block. The result must be trimmed with a razor so that the specimen protrudes from the block in a pyramid about one or two millimeters in cross section. The block is then mounted in a microtome and sliced with a diamond or glass knife into sections that are from 150 Å to about 800 Å thick. The sections are floated on a water reservoir in the knife, called a boat. The EM grids are slipped under the sections and dried. The sections are stained again by floating the grids on drops of uryanol acetate and lead citrate. The grids are then rinsed and dried. They are now ready to be observed in the electron microscope.

References

1. Campbell, K.J., and Sandler, S.S. "Determination of Large Masses of Ground Ice in Permafrost." Billerica, Mass.: Geophysical Survey Systems, Inc., Technical Mem. 001-72, Jan. 1972.

2. Cosslett, V.E. *Modern Microscopy*. Ithaca, N.Y.: Cornell University Press, 1966.

3. Ferrians, O.J., Jr. *Permafrost Map of Alaska*. U.S. Geological Survey Miscellaneous Geological Inventories Map I-445, 1965.

4. Gregory, R.L. *Eye and Brain*. New York: McGraw-Hill Book Company, 1973.

5. Slayter, E.M. *Optical Methods in Biology*. New York: Wiley-Interscience, 1970.

6. Sterns, S.R. "Permafrost (Perenially Frozen Ground)." U.S.A. Cold Region Research Engineering Laboratory Monograph 1-A2, 1966.

7. Vaiana, G.S.; Davis, J.M.; Giacconi, R.; Krieger, A.S.; Silk, J.K.; Timothy, A.M.; and Zombech, M. "X-ray Observations of Characteristic Structures and Time Variations from the Solar Corona: Preliminary Results from Skylab." *Astrophysics Journal*, vol. 185 (1973), L47.

8. Vaiana, G.S.; Krieger, A.S.; Petrasso, R.; Silk, J.K.; and Timothy, A.M. "The X-ray Spectrographic Telescope." *Instrumentation in Astronomy II. Proceedings of the Society of Photo-optical Instrument Engineers*. Tucson, Ariz., 1974, p. 185.

9. Vaiana, G.S.; Krieger, A.S.; and Timothy, A.M. "Identification and Analysis of Structures in the Corona from X-ray Photography." *Solar Physics*, vol. 32 (1973), pp. 81-116.

2 Transmission Pictures

A photograph taken on the electron microscope described in Chapter 1 is a good example to use for a transmission picture. The characteristics of these pictures are also found in many other types of transmission pictures. The structure of a biological specimen as observed in an electron micrograph appears to be relatively free of sharp boundaries. Sometimes a close examination of an electron micrograph may confuse rather than enlighten. A more distant visual examination allows the local irregularities of the picture to disappear. The dominant characteristics that remain give the visual sensation of a physical structure. The representation of a general structure is shown diagrammatically in Figure 2-1. Note that the structure is designated by assigning a density number to every point in the object space. The magnitude of the numbers can be scaled to the densities in the space. For example, high numbers would correspond to high densities, and low numbers to the absence of matter. The numbers also represent a gray scale with high numbers corresponding to black, and low numbers to white. Mathematically, each point in space is numbered by the triplet (x, y, z). The density value ρ is a fourth dimension that is visualized by shading the region near the point (x, y, z) with the value of gray that corresponds to the density number. The shorthand notation $\rho(x, y, z)$ symbolizes the structure within the range of values of x, y, and z relevant to the specimen.

An abstraction of a specimen in an electron-microscope column is shown in Figure 2-2. The general cylindrical shape of the cross section can be deformed to a rectangular cross section to represent a thin slice of an embedded biological material. The ability to rotate the specimen in the EM column is due to an attachment called a goniometer. Mechanical controls are available that allow the specimen to be aligned along any preassigned axis. Figure 2-2 shows a specimen that has its long axis aligned along the z direction. The beam can be considered to consist of parallel bundles of electrons that are at right angles to the z direction. The beam goes through the specimen and then is recorded on a photographic plate. The variation in density on the photographic plate corresponds to the two-dimensional distribution of densities in the specimen. The three-dimensional object can be reduced to a set of two-dimensional slices that are stacked along the z axis. Each slice corresponds to a single line or stripe on the photograph. Figure 2-3 shows the geometry for a single slice. The projection values are plotted along the projection line on a scale that would be perpendicular to

31

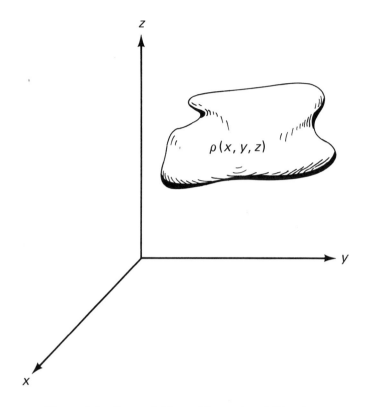

Figure 2-1. General Three-Dimensional Structure

the EM plate. Each projection point is calculated by summing the densities along the line of the EM beam. The discrete form for this process is

$$\sum_j \rho(\xi_j, \eta_i) = P_i(\eta_i) \tag{2.1}$$

The continuous form is

$$\int_{S_0(\eta_i)}^{S_f(\eta_i)} \rho(\xi, \eta_i) \, d\xi = P_i(\eta_i) \tag{2.2}$$

Consider the cylindrical disc cross section of Figure 2-4. Application of equation 2.2 for a beam that is in the y direction yields

$$\int_{-\sqrt{a^2-x^2}}^{\sqrt{a^2-x^2}} \rho(x, y) \, dy = P(x) \tag{2.3}$$

As an example of an application of equation 2.3, consider the projection

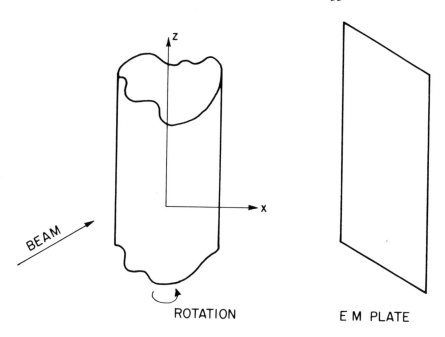

Figure 2-2. Geometry for Projecting a Transparent Object

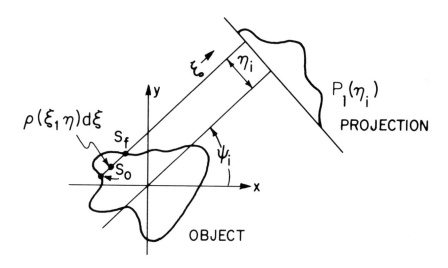

Figure 2-3. Geometry for a Single Slice

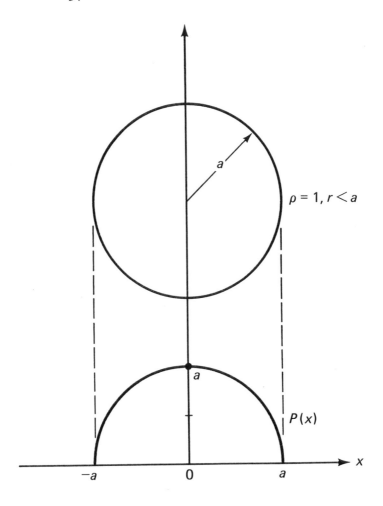

Figure 2-4. Solid Disc of Uniform Density and the Corresponding Projection

of a solid disc that has $\rho(x, y) = 1$. The result from 2.3, after integration, is

$$P(x) = 2\sqrt{a^2 - x^2} \qquad (2.4)$$

Figure 2-4 shows the density and projection distributions. Note that the projection has the same amplitude distribution independent of the direction of the incident illumination. Objects may have densities that have both radial and azimuthal dependence. Later it will become more convenient merely to associate a number for each point in the density space. However, much insight into the understanding of pictures can be gained by first examining some idealized cases with functional relations for the densities.

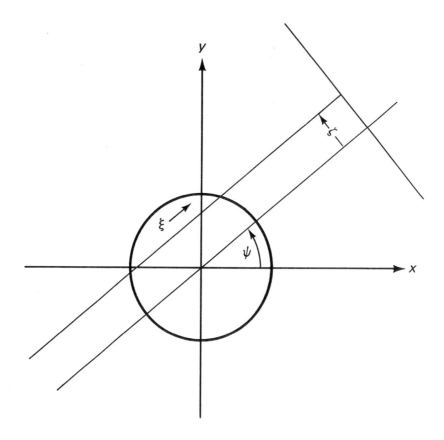

Figure 2-5. Object with Circular Cross Section

A geometry that is relevant to a rotated object with a circular cross section is shown in Figure 2-5. The generalized projection equation 2.2 can be specialized by finding the actual limits of integration and the explicit form of the kernel for any value of tilt angle ψ. The limits are calculated by finding the intersection of the straight lines, representing the beam direction, with the circular boundary. Consider the case where the density distribution is stationary and the coordinate axis is rotated through an angle ψ. The equation for the beam lines is

$$y = x \tan\psi + \eta/\cos\psi \qquad (2.5)$$

The equation for the circular boundary is

$$y = \pm\sqrt{a^2 - x^2} \qquad (2.6)$$

A simultaneous solution for equations 2.5 and 2.6 yields for the initial or final values

$$x = \eta \sin \psi \mp \cos \psi \sqrt{a^2 - \eta^2} \qquad (2.7)$$

The differential along the beam direction $d\xi$ is

$$dx\sqrt{1 + (dy/dx)^2} = \sec \psi \, dx \qquad (2.8)$$

Defining S_0 and S_f as the two solutions given by equation 2.7, the final form for the integral equation is

$$\int_{S_0}^{S_f} \rho(x, \, x \tan \psi + \eta/\cos \psi) \sec \psi \, dx = P(\eta) \qquad (2.9)$$

A simple positive function with angular dependence only is

$$\rho = |\cos n\phi| = |\cos[n(\tan^{-1}y/x)]| \qquad (2.10)$$

The plot of 2.10 for $n = 1$ is shown in Figure 2-6. Note that the density is constant along any radial line. A series of projection pictures corresponding to 2.10 with $n = 0, 1, 2,$ and 3 for various incident beam angles is shown in Figure 2-7. Figure 2-8 shows some corresponding pictures for cloverleaf patterns.[a] One of the basic conclusions that may be drawn from Figures 2-7 and 2-8 is that a single projection does not uniquely define a density distribution. The reader is encouraged to sketch equivalent density distributions that will give rise to the same projections as those shown in Figures 2-7 and 2-8.

The previous examples have concentrated on understanding idealized problems in picture processing, using artificial data. The data were of necessity quite smooth, since the density distributions were constructed from continuous mathematical functions. Real data have only a superficial relation to the idealized case. However, a beginning must be made somewhere. Actual data are considered to form a digitized set of numbers that are made available to the computer by processing the picture with an optical scanning instrument [1]. The instruments in general use are microdensitometers, flying-spot, and T.V. (or video) scanners. The instruments also may be described as either image- or object-plane scanners.

Figures 2-9a and b show the optical system of object- and image-plane scanners. The microdensitometer or object-plane scanner uses Koehler illumination. This system projects a uniformly illuminated field aperture onto the object plane. The object is imaged onto a photomultiplier detector by a conjugate optical system. The conjugate optical system consists of an objective lens, slit aperture, and a relay or Fabry lens. The scanner instrument in Figure 2-9b has a moving light spot. This spot is usually generated on the face of a cathode-ray tube (CRT) and is imaged on the film plane by an objective lens. The wanted section of film is imaged by a relay lens onto the photomultiplier detector.

[a] These patterns are due to Daniel Raemer.

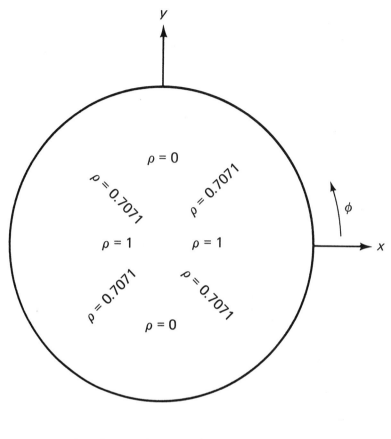

$$\rho(x, y) = |\cos[m(\tan^{-1} y/x)]|$$

Figure 2-6. Density Distribution for Sample Angularly Dependent Distribution

The microdensitometer is available as either a flat bed or a drum scanner. The flat-bed instrument can accommodate both film and glass plates. The drum scanner accommodates only film because the sample must be mounted on a rotating cylindrical drum. The flying-spot instruments are produced only in the flat-bed model.

The T.V. scanner is the optical inverse of the flying-spot scanner shown in Figure 2-9b. The phototube is replaced by a lamp. The film plane is uniformly illuminated by this lamp through a condenser lens. The illuminated object is then imaged onto the face of a vidicon using a second objective lens.

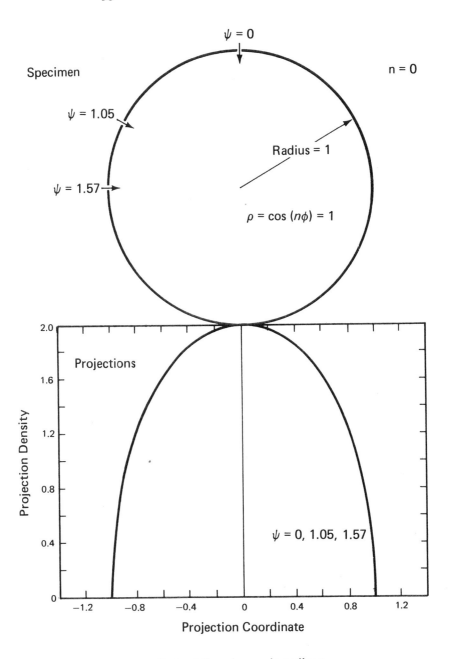

Note: All angles are in radians.

Figure 2-7a. Projection of Circular Specimen, Density = cos(nφ), n = 0

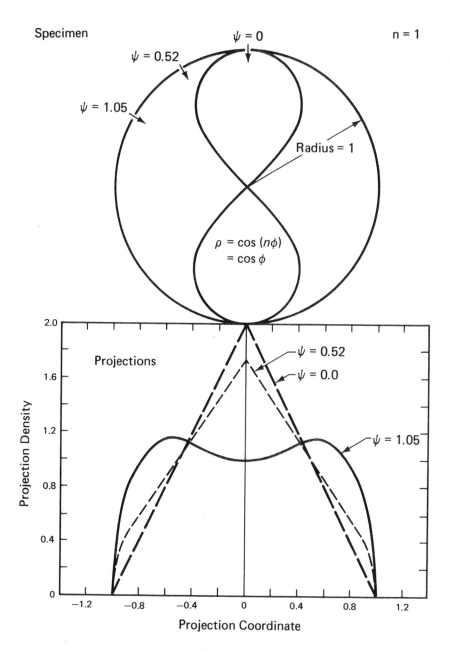

Figure 2-7b. Projection of Circular Specimen, Density $= \cos(n\phi)$, $n = 1$

40

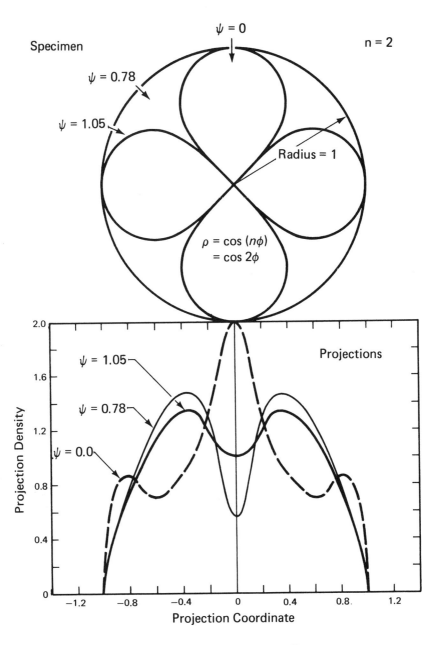

Figure 2-7c. Projection of Circular Specimen, Density = cos(nφ), n = 2

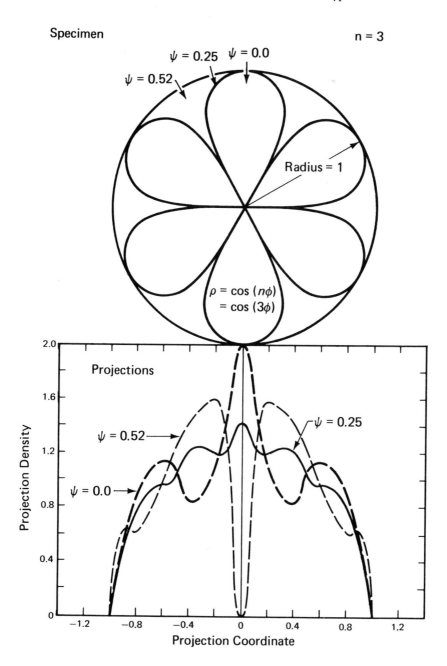

Figure 2-7d. Projection of Circular Specimen, Density $= \cos(n\phi)$, $n = 3$

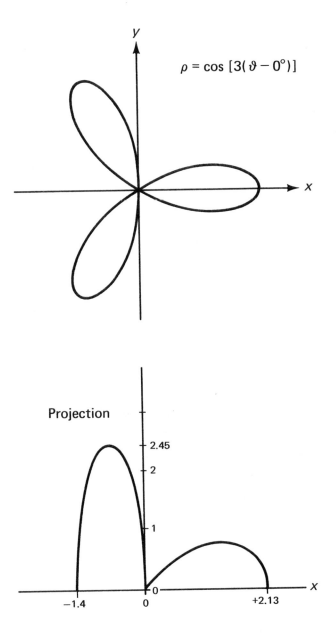

Figure 2-8a. Cloverleaf Projections from Different Angles, $\rho = \cos[3(\theta - 0)]$

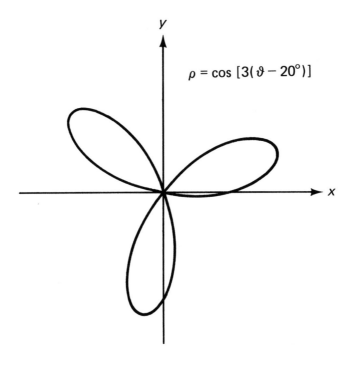

$$\rho = \cos\,[3(\vartheta - 20°)]$$

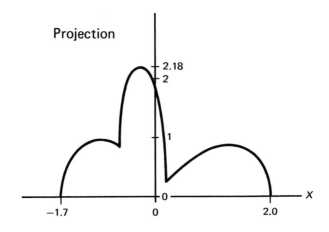

Projection

Figure 2-8b. Cloverleaf Projections from Different Angles, $\rho = \cos[3(\theta - 20)]$

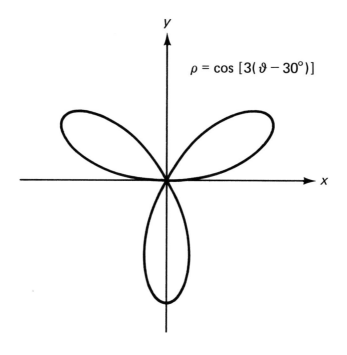

$$\rho = \cos\left[3(\vartheta - 30°)\right]$$

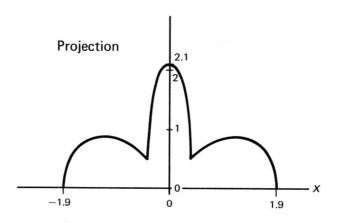

Projection

2.1

2

1

0

−1.9   0   1.9

x

Figure 2-8c. Cloverleaf Projections from Different Angles, $\rho = \cos[3(\theta - 30)]$

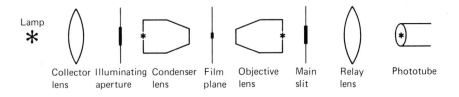

| Collector lens | Illuminating aperture | Condenser lens | Film plane | Objective lens | Main slit | Relay lens | Phototube |

Source: Miller, C.S.; Kofsky, I.L.; Trowbudge, C.A.; and Parsons, F.G. "Microdensitometers, 'Film Scanners,' and the EDP Scanning Microscope." *Optical Engineering*, vol. 12, no. 6 (1973).

Figure 2-9a. Characteristic Microdensitometer Optics

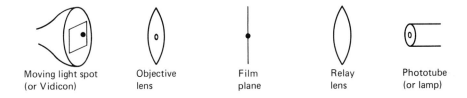

| Moving light spot (or Vidicon) | Objective lens | Film plane | Relay lens | Phototube (or lamp) |

Source: Miller, C.A.; Kofsky, I.L.; Trowbudge, C.A.; and Parsons, F.G. "Microdensitometers, 'Film Scanners,' and the EDP Scanning Microscope." *Optical Engineering*, vol. 12, no. 6 (1973).

Figure 2-9b. Characteristic Scanner Optics

A sample output for the microdensitometer instrument of Figure 2-9c (EDP Scanning Microscope) is shown in Figure 2-9d. This output was printed out in real time on the instrument. Both continuous time and (or) contoured plots are available. This microdensitometer has a spiral transport system with a sampling rate of 5 KHz. Apertures are available in the range of 1-800 microns. The eight-inch diameter real-time record contains up to 3 million data points and takes 10 minutes to produce.

A sample output from a flying-spot densitometer is shown in Figure 2-10a. The original picture is of a length of stacked-disc tobacco mosaic virus prepared by John Finch of the Medical Research Council in Cambridge, England, and is shown in Figure 2-10b. The sample output is for a section about five or six discs in length. A close examination of the original picture would show that the discs and the sub-units have a very fuzzy appearance. The densitometered output not only shows this soft appearance, but also contains noise added by the electronics of the densitometer. A visualization of the picture is made by assigning a gray level to each

Source: Miller, C.S.; Kofsky, I.L.; Trowbudge, C.A.; and Parsons, F.G. "Microdensitometers, 'Film Scanners,' and the EDP. Scanning Microscope." *Optical Engineering*, vol. 12, no. 6 (1973). Photograph courtesy of Photometrics, Inc., Lexington, Mass.

Figure 2-9c. The EDP Scanning Microscope, a Transmission and Reflection Microdensitometer with Spiral Film Transport (right) and Writeout (left) Stages

Source: Miller, C.S.; Kofsky, I.L.; Trowbudge, C.A.; and Parsons, F.G. "Microdensitometers, 'Film Scanners,' and the EDP. Scanning Microscope." *Optical Engineering*, vol. 12, no. 6 (1973). Photograph courtesy of Photometrics, Inc., Lexington, Mass.

Figure 2-9d. Continuous-tone (left) and Density-contoured (right) Representations of an Aerial Photograph of Rock Structures

```
22 19 30 22 26 14 17 12 10 15 21 26 19 45 60 53 51 49 56 51 49 40 30 51 44 38 35 31 44 44 70 51 45 44 49 61
19 26 26 35 19 14 10 12  8 37 21 19 30 30 40 33 42 19 15 14 12 12 15 24 19 21 30 22 21 21 35 42 44 53 44 35
37 24 24 28 37 38 26 28 37 21 33 28 30 26 33 31 17 15 12  7 12 10 21 19 26 40 22 17 26 10 14 21 40 53 42 58
35 21 47 49 61 63 58 53 31 45 37 30 26 33 33 14 30 38 35 35 31 28 28 24 28 31 45 30 31 38 22 47 28 38 28 53
40 44 33 42 65 72 53 49 51 40 45 49 35 30 30 40 42 33 38 65 35 19 37 24 35 30 45 30 31 47 28 42 42 40 54 51
31 35 31 21 42 30 12 31 31 31 40 38 37 35 31 40 22 42 65 70 38 45 51 28 40 35 30 49 58 56 42 65 54 63 54 49
24 24 28 28 28 10 12 10 17 10 28 19 26 33 38 45 47 22 33 51 30 42 33 26 42 40 33 38 33 56 49 58 53 63 60 68
54 44 42 28 24 21 26 33 15 12 26 15 21 24 31 47 17 33 38  8 42 30 42 26 42 26 40 26 49 40 58 42 65 44 60 58
58 47 35 31 22 47 45 30 15 38 49 38 33 53 47 37 22 17 12 35 17 21 28 45 49 21 30 37 31 54 58 31 28 24 33 58
33 21 30 24 33 70 45 28 42 45 40 47 60 72 54 67 68 58 63 42 30 33 37 33 44 49 45 49 51 54 74 53 45 67 49 47
33 35 37 15 15 15 31 35 30 30 31 60 65 63 74 60 58 45 74 30 33 42 47 42 30 40 40 40 40 54 51 45 56 51 54 63
30 47 35 33 21 17 19 19 14 17 19 26 35 37 31 37 31 17 10 12 26 28 24 30 26 28 15 24 30 35 45 44 47 51 37 58
28 28 28 35 38 35 24 42 31 22 45 33 19 24 37 19 21 10  7  8 19 12 17 10 17 12 17  8 28 21 14 21 22 44 54 61
38 31 47 51 54 44 51 60 70 54 31 49 44 42 51 49 44 35 22 47 56 22 45 37 30 22 30 22 30 22 44 42 53 51 49 56
44 30 45 40 51 63 72 65 60 45 40 51 53 40 42 51 40 58 45 42 56 60 63 61 51 42 51 40 58 45 35 53 56 56 76 51
44 35 14 14 28 24 44 49 26 21 19 42 42 19 40 40 51 47 49 68 68 60 33 35 40 54 45 45 49 63 53 54 60 74 77 63
33 28 19 21 21 12 15 17 17 26 22 35 28 28 30 28 22 35 21 22 28 26 38 31 22 38 21 40 40 44 40 56 54 56 51 49
53 45 33 28 35 21 22 21 31 26 15 21 24 31 26 15 21 24 31 19  8 19 12 12 14 24 19 10 26 28 21 22 49 58 53 56
37 49 47 26 28 53 21 22 30 30 31 35 42 35 31 42 19  8 22 30 21 21 10 24 31 30 28 37 44 31 44 54 49 51 53 56
35 42 31 21 33 42 19 17 26 31 35 40 40 45 40 35 31 30 28 21 30 24 35 26 35 21 31 60 60 74 31 38 37 49 53 67
24 19 28 21 19 22 22 28 26 26 31 37 37 33 40 33 44 40 40 37 45 35 58 54 28 42 21 31 40 26 44 40 53 47 49 74
22 19 21 19 17 22 30 28 30 33 30 31 31 44 31 44 42 17 35 33 22 15 26 24 42 24 22 21 40 26 33 44 42 49 53 56
30 33 30 35 28 38 19 19 31 33 33 54 37 33 44 30 35 31 53 30 26 24 15 26 30 30 26 24 35 40 45 26 45 42 53 54
49 65 74 47 28 40 42 35 54 54 31 53 30 26 45 26 40 42 54 67 56 45 38 31 31 31 26 21 26 45 49 44 54 61 63 58
37 60 45 56 35 33 42 40 54 44 44 30 67 56 45 53 31 31 31 31 44 40 54 53 58 61 54 58 63 54 63 58
```

Figure 2-10a. TMV Sample Densitometer Output

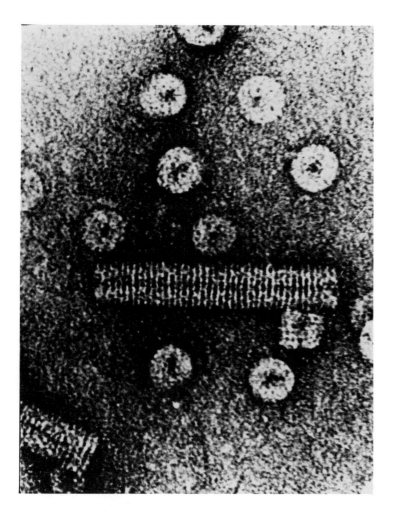

Photograph by John Finch, M.R.C., Cambridge, England.

Figure 2-10b. Electron Micrograph of Stacked-Disc TMV

number. The gray level is printed digitally with the higher numbers corresponding to the black range in the original picture. Note that the numbers are far from smooth as illustrated in Figure 2-11. The densities are always positive, with a nonzero background level. The output can be visualized in the same way that one views a picture. This requires the assignment of an optical density to each digital value. Figure 2-12a shows a hand-shaded output. The reader may find it helpful to defocus his eyes to improve the visual perception for the picture. A more sophisticated output is shown in Figure 2-12b. Here the original range of numbers (i.e., from 0 to 80) was divided by 5 to give 16 levels of gray. These levels were represented by a number of vertical strokes. The original picture is represented by an array of 25 by 35 rectangles. The rectangles are then filled with the proper density of vertical strokes. An out-of-focus picture of Figure 2-12b is shown in Figure 2-13. The out-of-focus picture is particularly good for giving the viewer an immediate representation similar to the original picture. The out-of-focus picture also has the advantage of not requiring the viewer's eye to be defocused.

The basic relation between the density distribution and the projection given in 2.2 involves an integration. It is convenient, both analytically and computationally to consider the representation of the integral by a sum. The Euler-Maclaurin sum formula provides this relation. It is

$$\int_{x_0}^{x_0+nh} f(x)\, dx = h[\tfrac{1}{2}f(x_0) + f(x_0 + h) + \ldots + f(x_0 + (n-1)h)$$

$$+ \tfrac{1}{2}f(x_0 + nh)] - \frac{B_2 h^2}{2!}\, [f'(x_0 + nh) - f'(x_0) \ldots]\ (2.11)$$

where n = number of points

h = incremental length

B_2 = Bernoulli number

f' = derivative of $f(x)$ with respect to x

A first approximation for 2.11 that is useful for programming and analysis is the rectangular integration approximation. The approximation involves only constant coefficients, and is given by

$$\int_{x_0}^{x_0+nh} f(x)\, dx \cong h[f(x_0) + f(x_0 + h) + \ldots$$

$$+ f(x_0 + (n-1)h) + f(x_0 + nh)]\qquad (2.12)$$

The approximate value for the projected image for a circular disc of uniform density can be computed from 2.12. A three-point formula which takes advantage of the symmetry in the half planes yields

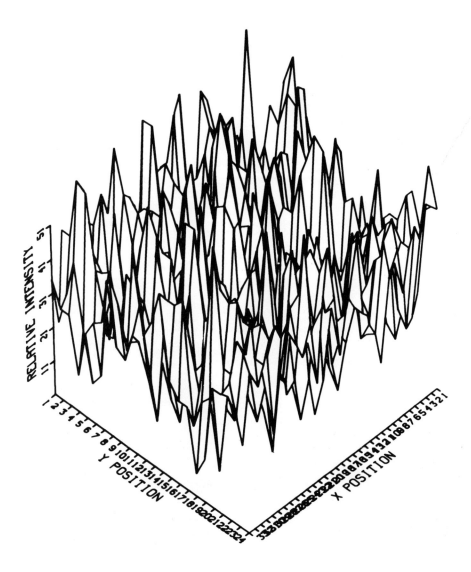

Figure 2-11. A Three-Dimensional Representation of a Section of the Densitometered Output of Figure 2-10a

$$\int_{-\sqrt{a^2-x^2}}^{\sqrt{a^2-x^2}} \rho(x,\, y)\, dy \;=\; \int_{-\sqrt{a^2-x^2}}^{\sqrt{a^2-x^2}} 1 \cdot dy = 2 \cdot \frac{\sqrt{a^2 - x^2}}{2}\, \{1 + 1 + 1\}$$

$$= 3\sqrt{a^2 - x^2} \qquad\qquad (2.13)$$

52

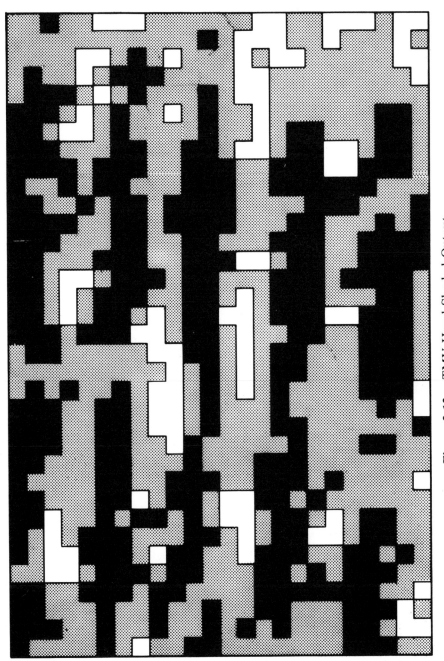

Figure 2-12a. TMV Hand Shaded Output

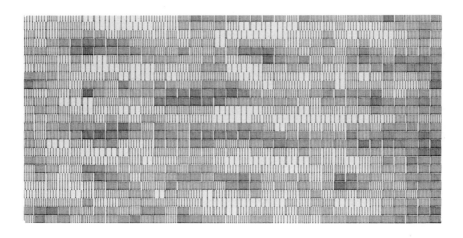

Figure 2-12b TMV Computer Shaded Output

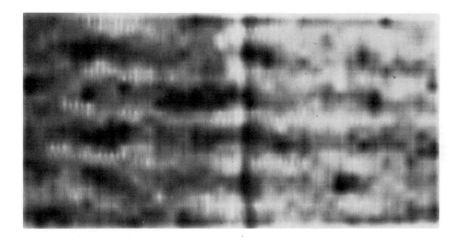

Figure 2-13. Out-of-Focus Picture of Figure 2.12b

The exact value for 2.13 is

$$\int_{-\sqrt{a^2-x^2}}^{\sqrt{a^2-x^2}} 1 \cdot dy = 2\sqrt{a^2 - x^2} \tag{2.14}$$

The accuracy for the rectangular integration formula can be improved by increasing the number of terms. The 11- and 111-point formulas yield, respectively

$$\int_{-\sqrt{a^2-x^2}}^{\sqrt{a^2-x^2}} 1 \cdot dy \simeq 2.20\sqrt{a^2 - x^2} \qquad (2.15)$$

and

$$\int_{-\sqrt{a^2-x^2}}^{\sqrt{a^2-x^2}} 1 \cdot dy \simeq 2.018\sqrt{a^2 - x^2} \qquad (2.16)$$

Note that the error in using 2.16 is less than one percent compared to 2.14.

Transmission pictures can be examined for structural order. They can be used to determine the basic geometrical lengths in the projection picture and in the original structure. It will be useful in discussing ideas associated with order perception to define a point-density function that is analogous to the mathematical delta or Dirac delta function. The properties of the delta function $\delta(x)$ are

$$\delta(x) = \begin{cases} 0, x \neq 0 \\ \\ \infty, x = 0 \end{cases} \qquad (2.17)$$

$$\int_{-\infty}^{\infty} \delta(x)\, dx = 1 \qquad (2.18)$$

$$\int_{-\infty}^{\infty} \delta(x)\, f(x)\, dx = f(0) \qquad (2.19)$$

Consider the one-dimensional point-density function with value ρ_0 located at $x = x'$. The density is represented mathematically by

$$\rho_0 \cdot \delta(x - x') \qquad (2.20)$$

The density has the property from 2.19 that

$$\int_X \rho_0\, \delta(x - x')\, dx' = \rho_0 \qquad (2.21)$$

where

$$x' \in X \qquad (2.22)$$

This last property merely states that the point density is located within the range of integration in 2.21. A two-dimensional array of point densities is represented by a double summation of delta functions. The mathematical form for the array of Figure 2-14 is

$$\rho(x,y) = \sum_m \sum_n \delta(x - md_1)\, \delta(y - nd_2) \qquad (2.23)$$

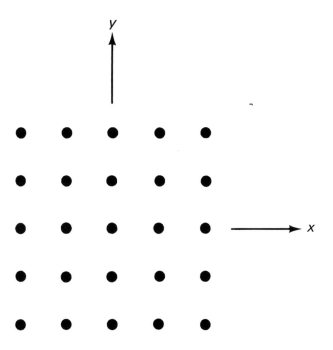

Figure 2-14. Square Array of Spots

The transmission picture equation corresponding to 2.23 is given by 2.2.

$$\int_{S_0}^{S_f} \sum_m \sum_n \delta(x - md_1)\,\delta(y - nd_2)\,dy = P(x) \qquad (2.24)$$

$$N \sum_m \delta(x - md_1) = P(x) \qquad (2.25)$$

The constant N represents the number of density points along the y direction in the range from S_0 to S_f, using equation 2.18. The projection line corresponding to Figure 2-14 is shown in Figure 2-15. The line on a photograph is sketched in Figure 2-15 as a series of black dots. A transmission picture that is taken of the rotated sections of the array of Figure 2-14 is easily represented by the rotation integral 2.9 with 2.23 or

$$P(\eta) = \int_{S_0}^{S_f} \sum_m \sum_n \delta(x - md_1)\,\delta\!\left(x \tan\psi + \frac{\eta}{\cos\psi} - nd_2\right)\sec\psi\,dx \qquad (2.26)$$

The conditions for the appearance of a projection point are determined by making both delta-function arguments in 2.26 equal to zero. They are

$$x - md_1 = 0 \qquad (2.27)$$

Figure 2-15. Projection of Square Array of Spots

$$x \tan \psi + \eta/\cos \psi - nd_2 = 0 \qquad (2.28)$$

The simultaneous solution for 2.27 and 2.28 is

$$\eta = \eta_{m,n} = nd_2 \cos \psi - md_1 \sin \psi \qquad (2.29)$$

The relation 2.29 is a very important result that gives the discrete values along the projection line for the occurrence of spots. Thus, for a given set of distances d_1 and d_2, and rotation angle ψ, a number of spots occurs corresponding to particular values of m and n. Consider the example of a 3×3 array shown in Figure 2-16. Here $d_1 = d_2 = 1$. Two examples are considered: Case I, $\psi = \pi/4$; and Case II, $\psi = \pi/6$. The results are summarized in Table 2-1.

The preceding method can be very useful for checking for the occurrence of spots for a predetermined lattice. Another example is shown in Figure 2-17, in which a hexagonal lattice is resolved into two square lattices.

The point densities for a hexagonal array can be represented by a decomposition into two sub-arrays, each having a square lattice (see Figure 2-17). Mathematically, one array involves even indices and the other odd. If the smallest square size is d, then the density for the original hexagonal lattice $\rho_h(x,y)$ is given by

$$\rho_h(x,y) = \sum_{\substack{m,n \\ \text{even}}} \delta(x - md)\,\delta(y - nd) + \sum_{\substack{m,n \\ \text{odd}}} \delta(x - md)\,\delta(y - nd) \qquad (2.30)$$

A good example of the use of 2.30 is given by the projection pictures of insect flight muscle. The structure of insect flight muscle consists of a parallel array of myosin and actin filaments, which are connected by cross-bridges. The myosin filaments are larger in diameter (about 400 Å) than the actin filaments (about 120 Å). The distance between the layers of actin and myosin is about 200 Å. The thick sections cut from the flight muscle of the lethocearus used by Reedy are generally about 400 or 500 Å in width. They include both actin and myosin layers. Generally they have one actin layer and two myosin layers, or one myosin and two actin layers. The sections were tilted about the long axis of the filaments using a goniometer. The pictures for various angles of tilt are shown in Figures 2-18a, b, c, d, and e. Note the basic repetition of the pictures after a total tilt of 60 degrees. This effect is due to properties inherent to the hexagonal structure of the

Table 2-1
Projections for 3×3 Array at Two Different Tilt Angles.

Case I: tilt angle $\psi = \pi/4$, $d_1 = d_2 = 1$				$\eta_{m,n} = (\sqrt{2}/2)(n - m)$	

n \ m	-1	0	1	
1	$\sqrt{2}$	$\sqrt{2}/2$	0	
0	$\sqrt{2}/2$	0	$-\sqrt{2}/2$	η location of projection points
-1	0	$-\sqrt{2}/2$	$-\sqrt{2}$	

Case II: tilt angle $\psi = \pi/6$, $d_1 = d_2 = 1$				$\eta_{m,n} = (1/2)(\sqrt{3}n - m)$	

n \ m	-1	0	1	
1	1.366	0.866	0.366	
0	0.5	0	-0.5	η location of projection points
-1	-0.366	-0.866	-1.366	

filaments. The basic effect in the pictures can be explained using equation 2.30. Thus, for the model of Figure 2-17, the densities for the myosin muscle filament are represented by

$$\rho(x,y) = \sum_{\substack{m \\ \text{even}}} \sum_{n=-2} \delta(x - md)\,\delta(y - nd) + \sum_{\substack{m \\ \text{odd}}} \delta(x - md) \qquad (2.31)$$

The tilted picture is obtained by replacing y in 2.31 according to 2.5. The result is a series of two spots (or lines in the three-dimensional case). The first set produces lines according to 2.9, or at

$$\eta_{m,e} = d(n \cos \psi - m \sin \psi) \qquad (2.32)$$

The above relation corresponds to the first sum on the right of 2.31 and the second series of lines comes from the second sum on the right. Since $x = \eta/\sin\psi$, the lines occur at

$$\eta_{m,o} = x \sin \psi = md \sin \psi \qquad (2.33)$$

The cases corresponding to tilts of $\psi = \pm 30°$ are summarized below:

Case I: $\qquad\qquad \psi = 30°$

$$\eta_{m,e} = d(n \cos \pi/6 - m \sin \pi/6)$$

$$\eta_{m,o} = md \sin \pi/6$$

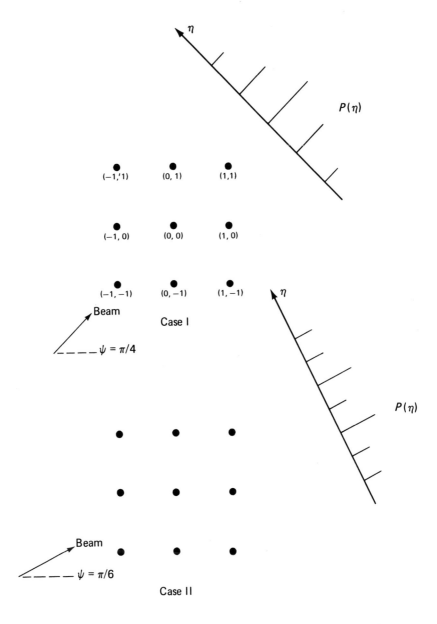

Figure 2-16. Projection of Array from Two Different Angles

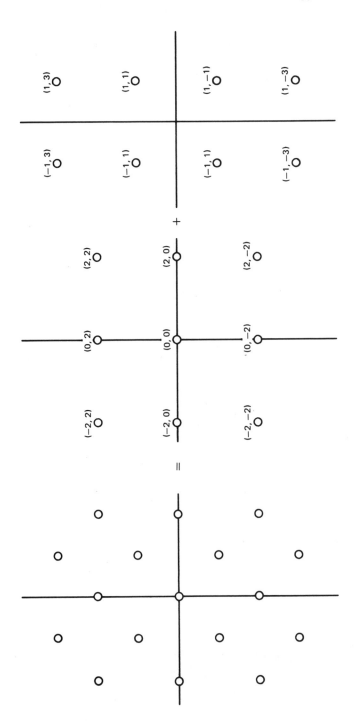

Figure 2-17. Decomposition of Hexogonal Array into Two Rectangular Arrays

Photograph by Michael Reedy.

Figure 2-18a. Electron Micrograph of Insect Flight Muscle Taken at Different Rotation Angles. Rotation Angle Is 38°.

Photograph by Michael Reedy.

Figure 2-18b. Rotation angle Is 15°

Figure 2-18c. Rotation Angle Is −3 1/2°

Photograph by Michael Reedy.

Figure 2-18d. Rotation Angle is −15°

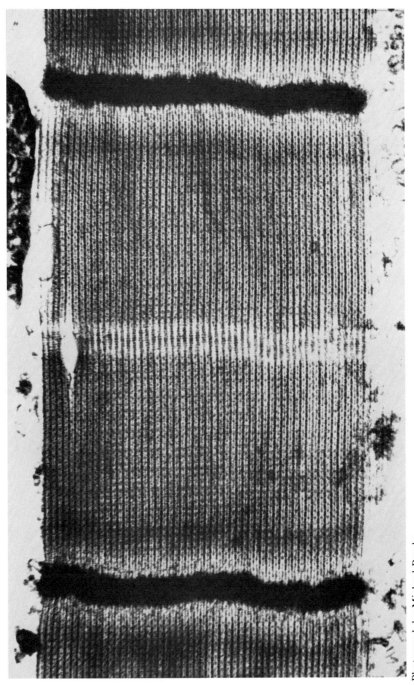

Figure 2-18e. Rotation Angle Is −33°

Photograph by Michael Reedy.

Case II: $\qquad \psi = -30°$

$$\eta_{m,e} = d(n \cos \pi/6 + m \sin \pi/6)$$

$$\eta_{m,o} = -md \sin \pi/6$$

A good example of a continuous structure is the helix. The helical structure is quite common in biology, appearing sometimes as the backbone for a complicated molecular arrangement. The helix may be described mathematically by the parametric equations

$$\left. \begin{array}{l} x = a \cos \phi \\ y = a \sin \phi \\ z = a \tan \alpha \cdot \phi \end{array} \right\} \quad 0 \leqq \phi \leqq 2\pi \qquad (2.34)$$

where $\quad a =$ radius of the helix

$\qquad \alpha =$ pitch of the helix

The angle y in 2.34 is the azimuthal coordinate for a cylindrical system. The helix described by 2.34 is wound about the z axis. The helix may be represented as a three-dimensional density function by considering it as a line with a delta-function density. Viewing the helix along the x-axis, the last two equations of 2.34 combine to give the one equation

$$\frac{z}{a \tan \alpha} = \sin^{-1} y/a \qquad (2.35a)$$

or

$$y = a \sin (z/(a \tan \alpha)) \qquad (2.35b)$$

The representation for the delta-function density is easily obtained from 2.35. It is

$$\rho(y,z) = \delta[y - a \sin (z/(a \tan \alpha))] \qquad (2.36)$$

The projection of the helix due to a source parallel to the x axis is the line described by making the argument of the delta function equal to zero. The projection is a sine wave traced along the z axis.

The rotation picture generated by rotating the helix about the y axis is given by again projecting the figure on a plane perpendicular to the x axis. The coordinate system for the helix is primed, and the original coordinate system is unprimed. The relation between the primed and unprimed system is

$$z = z' \cos \theta - x' \sin \theta$$

$$x = z' \sin \theta + x' \sin \theta \qquad (2.37)$$

$$y = y'$$

The parametric equations for the helix in the rotated frame are given by 2.34 with x and z replaced by x' and z', respectively. The new parametric equations for the helix in the original frame are

$$x = a \cos \phi \cos \theta + (a \tan \alpha) \phi \sin \theta$$

$$y = a \sin \phi \qquad (2.38)$$

$$z = -a \cos \phi \sin \theta + (a \tan \alpha) \phi \cos \theta$$

where θ = rotation angle.

Viewing along the y-axis, the first and third equations of 2.38 combine to give the following transcendental relation, which describes the helix in the frame of the unprimed coordinate system

$$\cos \left(\frac{x \sin \theta + z \cos \theta}{a \tan \alpha} \right) = \frac{1}{a} (x \cos \theta - z \sin \theta) \qquad (2.39)$$

The corresponding representation for the delta-function density is

$$\delta \left[\cos \left(\frac{x \sin \theta + z \cos \theta}{a \tan \alpha} \right) - \frac{1}{a} (x \cos \theta - z \sin \theta) \right] \qquad (2.40)$$

A plot of the projection picture for a tilt of 30 degrees is given in Figure 2-19, along with the 0-degree projection.

Computer Generated Graphics of a Tilted Helix

The parametric equations for a helix tilted about the y axis by an angle θ are given by equation 2.38. The corresponding three-dimensional density function for an infinitesimally thin tilted helix is

$$\rho(x,y,z) = \delta[x - a \cos \phi \cos \theta - (a \tan \alpha) \phi \sin \theta] \cdot \delta(y - a \sin \phi)$$

$$\cdot \delta[z + a \cos \phi \sin \theta + (a \tan \alpha) \phi \cos \theta] \qquad (2.41)$$

The projection picture corresponding to the density of equation 2.41 is given by integrating $\rho(x,y,z)$ over the range of the x coordinate. The result is the projection $P(y,z)$. If the y and z delta-function arguments are simultaneously made equal to zero in 2.41, then

$$\rho(y,z) = \delta \left(\frac{z}{a} - \tan \alpha \cos \theta \left[\left(\sin^{-1} \frac{y}{a} \right) + 2n\pi \right] \right.$$

$$\left. - \sin \theta \cos \left(\sin^{-1} \frac{y}{a} \right) \right)$$

$$n = 0, \pm 1, \pm 2, \ldots \qquad (2.42)$$

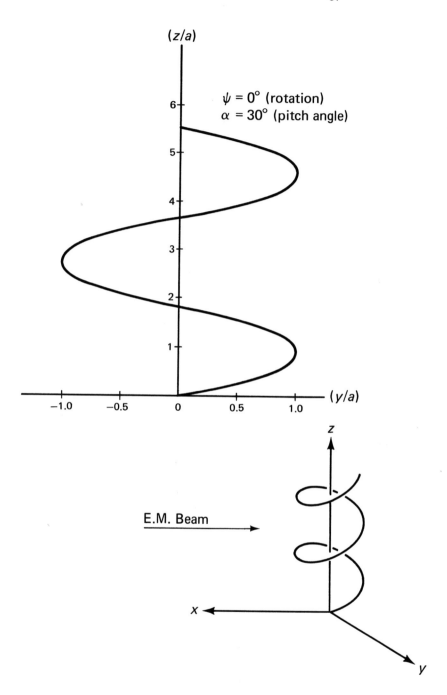

Figure 2-19a. Projection of a Helix

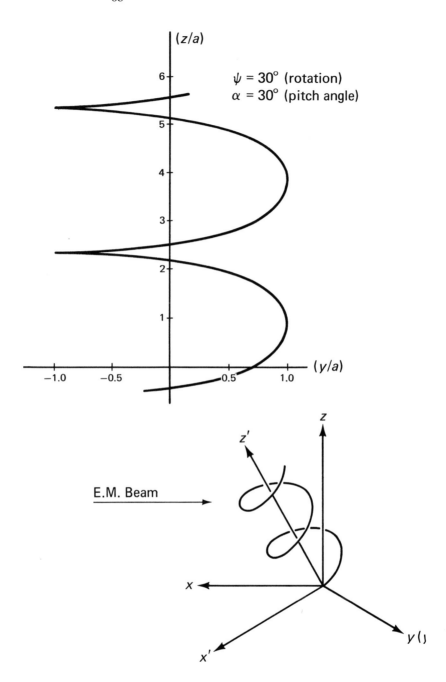

Figure 2-19b. Projection of a Rotated Helix

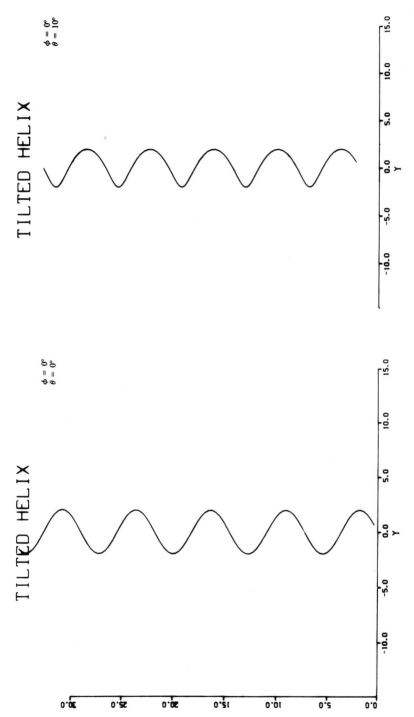

Figure 2-20. Projection Pictures of Helices, Different Values of θ, $\phi = 0°$

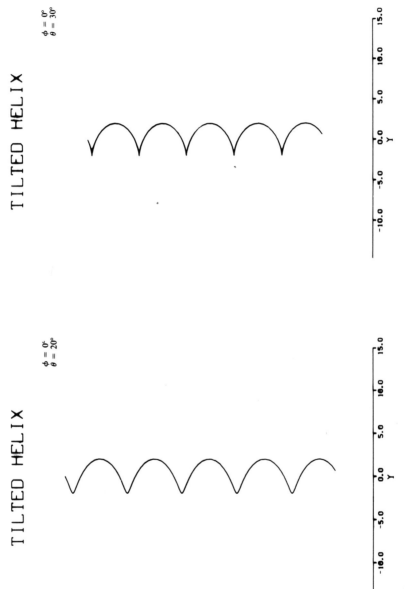

Figure 2-20. (Continued)

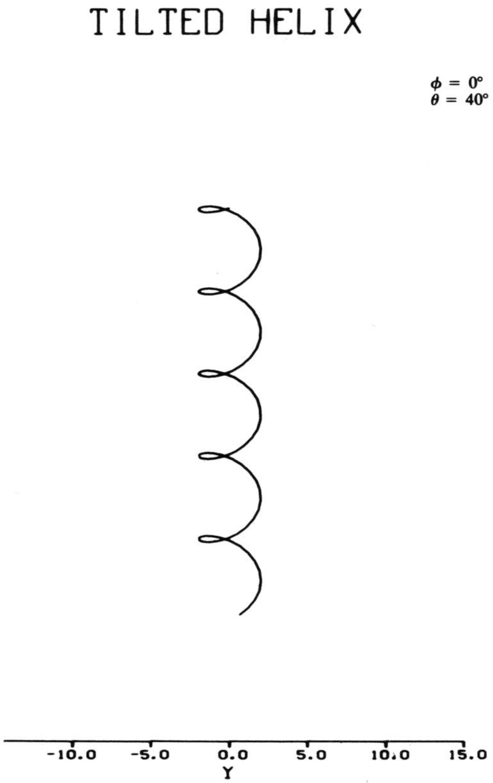

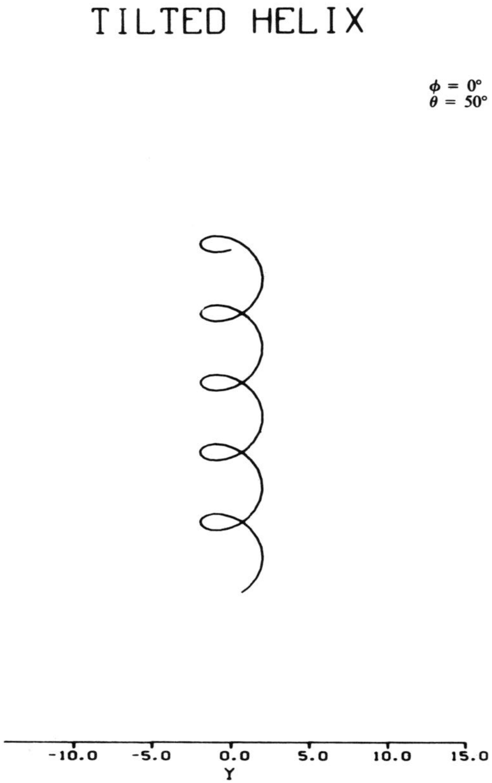

TILTED HELIX
$\phi = 0°$
$\theta = 40°$
-10.0 -5.0 0.0 5.0 10.0 15.0
Y

TILTED HELIX
$\phi = 0°$
$\theta = 50°$
-10.0 -5.0 0.0 5.0 10.0 15.0
Y

Figure 2-20. (Continued)

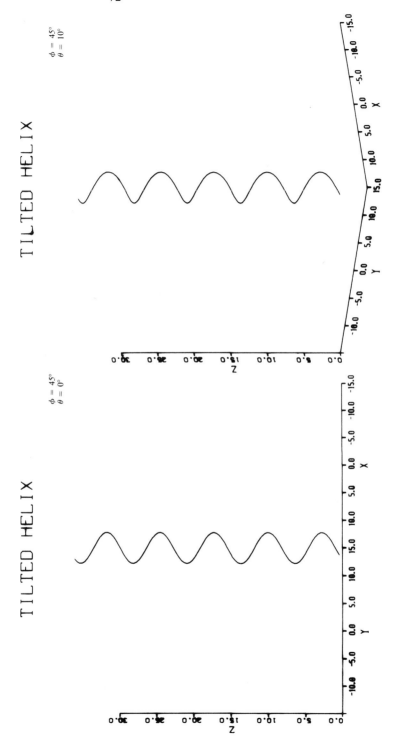

Figure 2-21. Projection Pictures of Helices, Different Values of θ, $\phi = 45°$

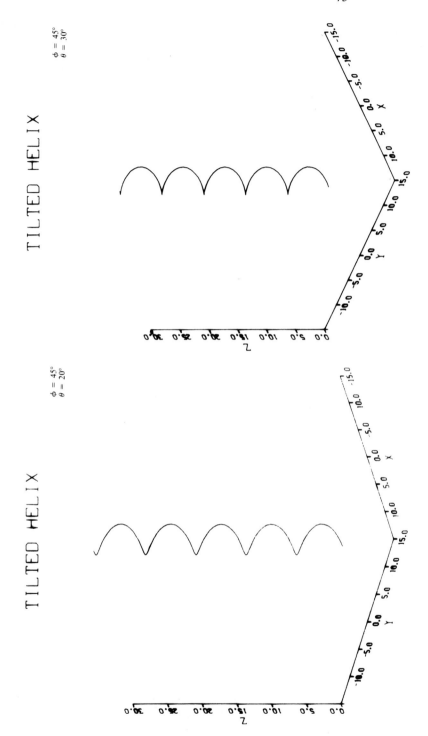

Figure 2-21. (Continued)

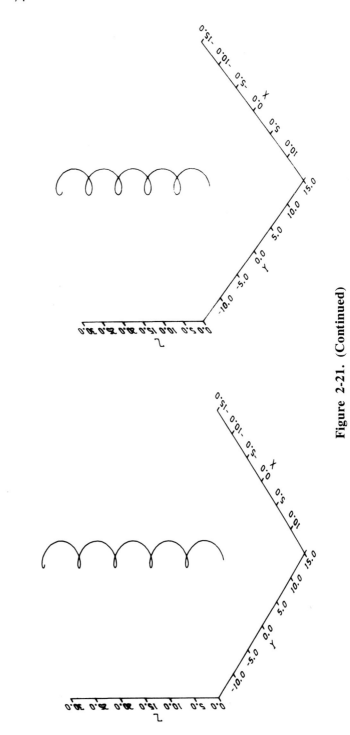

TILTED HELIX

$\phi = 45°$
$\theta = 50°$

TILTED HELIX

$\phi = 45°$
$\theta = 40°$

Figure 2-21. (Continued)

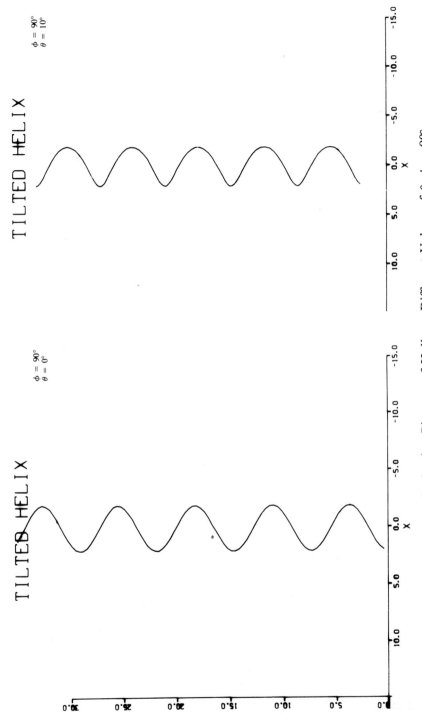

Figure 2-22. Projection Pictures of Helices, Different Values of θ, $\phi = 90°$

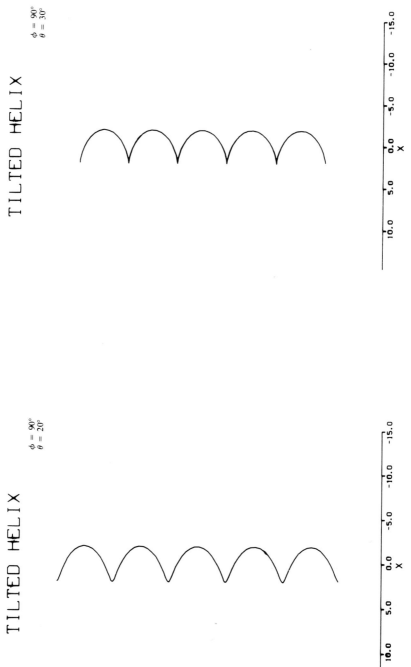

Figure 2-22. (Continued)

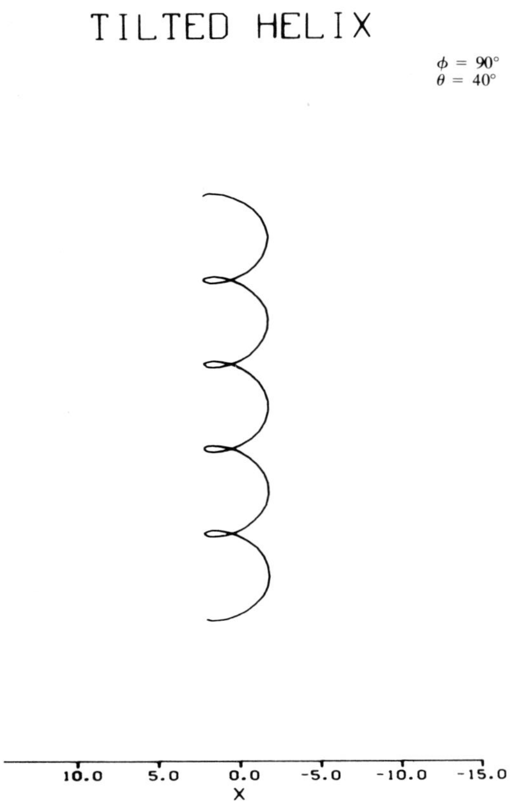

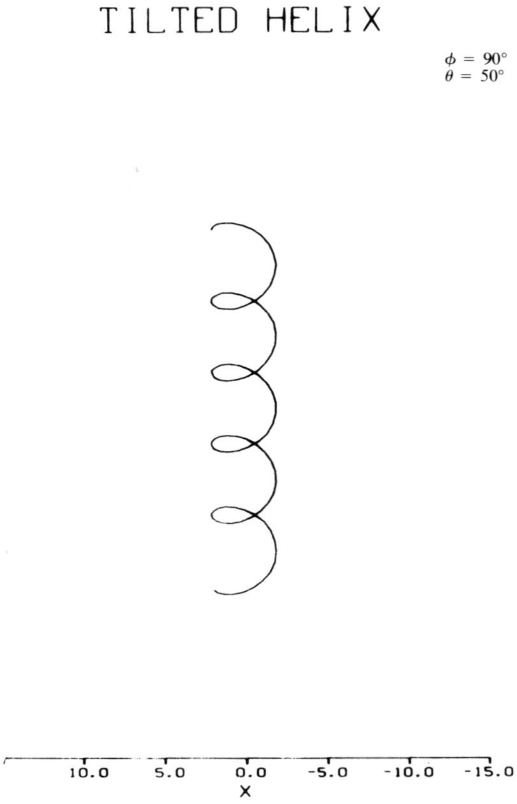

TILTED HELIX

$\phi = 90°$
$\theta = 50°$

TILTED HELIX

$\phi = 90°$
$\theta = 40°$

Figure 2-22. (Continued)

The standard practice in computer graphics is to write a general program for the projection of a three-space curve onto a two-dimensional "picture frame." A number of computer packages exist which perform the required calculations on an arbitrary curve. The transmission picture of a helix centered about the z axis was generated as a function of the rotation about the y axis. Note that the angle ϕ corresponds to a rotation about the z axis, and the angle θ is the tilt angle. Three sets of projections are presented for ϕ = 0°, 45°, and 90°. Six values of θ were plotted for each value of ϕ. They are θ = 0°, 10°, 20°, 30°, 40°, and 50°. These results are displayed in Figures 2-20, 2-21, and 2-22.[b]

Reference

1. Miller, C.S.; Kofsky, I.L.; Trowbridge, C.A.; and Parsons, F.G. "Microdensitometers, 'Film Scanners,' and the E.D.P. Scanning Microscope." *Optical Engineering*, vol. 12, no. 6 (1973), pp. 226-232.

---

[b]The results of this section are due to John Harrington.

3

The Optical Diffraction of Biological Pictures and Use of Fourier Methods for Gaining Structural Information

The occurrence of a particular type of order may not be readily apparent to the observer. Sometimes the order may occur as a repetiton of a basic length or as a basic lattice in the object. The order can easily occur simultaneously with a large, and usually masking, unordered component. The eye is quite biased, in the sense of preferring to make order out of disorder. Since the eye is prone to error in the type of order that it prefers, some objective method of discovering order is preferable. One such method is the use of optical diffraction or Fourier techniques. The primary use of these techniques is to discover the common distances among elements of an object and to give an indication of possible structural forms in the object. The operations involved in the use of these techniques may be performed either by computer or by the use of a diffractometer.

The optical transform or diffraction pattern of a two-dimensional projection picture is related to the Fourier transform of the picture. The optical diffraction pattern is easily obtained from a transparency of the picture by using a diffractometer as shown in Figure 3-1. A source, usually a laser beam, is placed at S_0. The picture is placed between the lenses L_1 and L_2. The diffraction pattern of the picture can then be observed or recorded at F. It will be shown later that the preceding optical process is mathematically equivalent to recording the intensity of the Fourier transformation of the picture. This transformation involves some of the usual processes in picture processing—digitalization of the picture for computer storage, for example. The computer-stored picture represents a two-dimensional function that can be used in the transformation integral.

The theory of diffraction has been well explained in the literature [1, 2]. A simplified treatment of optical diffraction will be given here. This treatment is sufficient for the small-angle diffraction phenomenon that is relevant to either laser-diffracted or computer-diffracted (i.e., transformed) patterns.

The basic geometry is shown in Figure 3-2. The picture is located in the x-y plane. The picture is framed by a perfectly opaque screen. A completely polarized source of light is located to the left. The diffraction pattern of the picture occurs at some point P which will be located at a large distance (in wavelengths) away from the picture.

The light intensity to the right of the screen of Figure 3-2 obeys the wave equation in free space. The wave equation for a harmonic source is

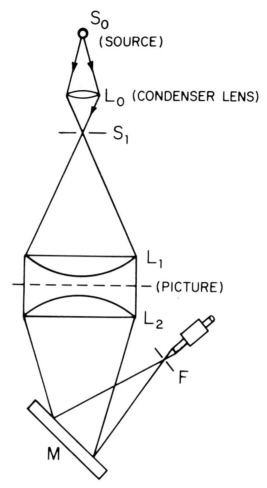

Source: Taylor, C.A., and Lipson, H. *Optical Transforms*. Ithaca, N.Y.: Cornell University Press, 1964, p. 30.

Figure 3-1. An Optical Diffractometer

$$(\nabla^2 + k_0^2)\, U_\delta(P) = -\rho(\mathbf{r}') \qquad (3.1)$$

where ∇^2 = Laplacian

$k_0 = 2\pi/\lambda_0$

λ_0 = wavelength

$\mathbf{r}'$ denotes the vector $\vec{r}'$

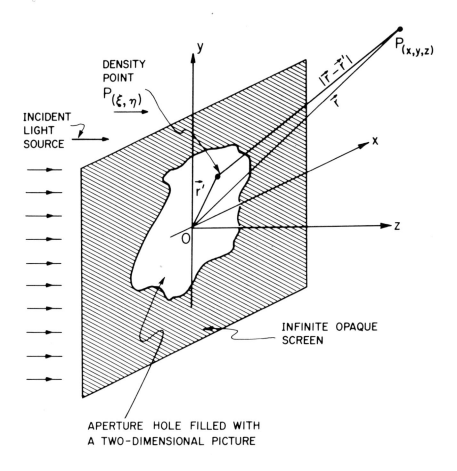

Figure 3-2. Picture Framed by Opaque Screen

The solution to equation 3.1 will be obtained from Huygen's principle, which states that the light intensity at point P is the superposition of all the elementary wavelets from all the distributed sources in the picture plane. This principle can be used to superimpose the light intensity from a delta-function source located at $\mathbf{r} = \mathbf{r}'$. The light intensity from a delta-function source $U_\delta(P)$ satisfies the equation

$$(\nabla^2 + k_0^2)\, U_\delta(P) = -\delta(\mathbf{r} - \mathbf{r}') \tag{3.2}$$

The solution to 3.2 is called the Green's function. The Green's function for 3.2 for a spherically symmetric source is

$$U_\delta = \frac{1}{4\pi} \frac{e^{-jk_0|\mathbf{r}-\mathbf{r}'|}}{|\mathbf{r}-\mathbf{r}'|} \qquad (3.3)$$

where $j = \sqrt{-1}$.

The solutions given by 3.3 for a delta-function source located at $\mathbf{r} = \mathbf{r}'$ can be superimposed by integration to yield the light intensity U for a distributed source located over a picture.

The scalar distance $|\mathbf{r} - \mathbf{r}'|$ between a point on the aperture plane $P(\xi, \eta)$ and a point in the diffraction plane $P(x, y, z)$ is

$$|\mathbf{r} - \mathbf{r}'| = [(x - \xi)^2 + (y - \eta)^2 + z^2]^{1/2} \qquad (3.4)$$

The distance $|\mathbf{r} - \mathbf{r}'|$ in equation 3.4 can be expanded in a way that is convenient for expansion of the square root as follows:

$$|\mathbf{r} - \mathbf{r}'| = [(x^2 + y^2 + z^2) + \xi^2 + \eta^2 - 2(\xi x + \eta y)]^{1/2}$$

$$= [r^2 + r'^2 - 2(\xi x + \eta y)]^{1/2}$$

$$|\mathbf{r} - \mathbf{r}'| = r\left[1 + \frac{r'^2}{r^2} - \frac{2(\xi x + \eta y)}{r^2}\right]^{1/2} \qquad (3.5)$$

where $r = |\mathbf{r}|, \quad r' = |\mathbf{r}'|$.

The diffraction plane specified by $P(x, y, z)$ is now assumed to be sufficiently far away so that

$$r'^2/r^2 \ll 1 \qquad (3.6)$$

and

$$2(\xi x + \eta y)/r^2 < 1 \qquad (3.7)$$

The conditions 3.6 and 3.7 allow the square root of 3.5 to be expanded in a convergent series. The result for this expansion is

$$|\mathbf{r} - \mathbf{r}'| = r - (\xi x + \eta y)/r + \text{higher order terms} \qquad (3.8)$$

where only the zeroth and first order terms are shown explicitly. Equation 3.8 may be further simplified by noting the following relations which involve the direction cosines of the diffraction point $P(x, y, z)$. These relations are

$$\alpha = x/r \qquad (3.9a)$$

and

$$\beta = y/r \qquad (3.9b)$$

Finally, the solution of 3.1 using the Green's function 3.3 within the approximation of 3.8 is

$$U = \int U_\delta(|\mathbf{r} - \mathbf{r}'|)\rho(\mathbf{r}')\,dr' \qquad (3.10a)$$

$$U(\alpha, \beta) = \frac{1}{4\pi}\frac{e^{-jk_0 r}}{r} \int_\xi \int_\eta \rho(\xi, \eta)e^{jk_0(\alpha\xi + \beta\eta)}\,d\xi\,d\eta \qquad (3.10b)$$

The diffraction picture $U(\alpha, \beta)$ is visualized in much the same way as an ordinary picture. The diffraction pattern is usually imaged on a photographic emulsion. The light and dark areas on the picture correspond to large and small values of the intensity I. I is given by

$$I = U(\alpha, \beta) \cdot U^*(\alpha, \beta) \qquad (3.11)$$

where $U^*(\alpha, \beta)$ is the complex conjugate. Note that 3.11 is *not* sufficient to determine U since the phase information is missing.

Specific Examples of the Diffraction of Transmission Pictures

The facility to interpret diffraction pictures can be acquired by a study of the results of representative ideal cases. Familiarity with a small number of basic configurations will supply a starting point for the understanding of more complex patterns. Usually it is not too difficult to gather the gross structural information from the diffraction pattern of a transmission picture. The fine structural detail is more difficult to determine. The following simplified cases illustrate some of the major effects seen in diffraction pictures. The densities and their diffraction patterns are illustrated in Figure 3-3. The intensity patterns are also shown in this figure.

1. A single point-density function at the origin is represented by

$$\rho(\xi, \eta) = \delta(\xi)\,\delta(\eta) \qquad (3.12)$$

The diffraction pattern is obtained by substituting 3.12 into 3.10b with the result

$$U(\alpha, \beta) = H \qquad (3.13)$$

where $\quad H = \text{constant} = \dfrac{1}{4\pi}\dfrac{e^{-jk_0 r}}{r}$

2. A line of finite length along the η axis with length η_0 is represented by

$$\rho(\xi, \eta) = \delta(\xi)\{H(\eta + \eta_0/2) - H(\eta - \eta_0/2)\} \qquad (3.14)$$

$\rho(\xi, \eta)$ $|\nu(\alpha, \beta)|$

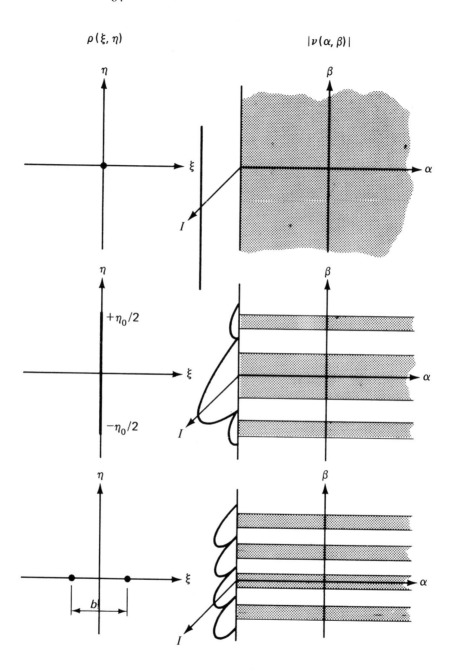

Figure 3-3. Two-Dimensional Density Distributions and Their Corresponding Diffraction Patterns

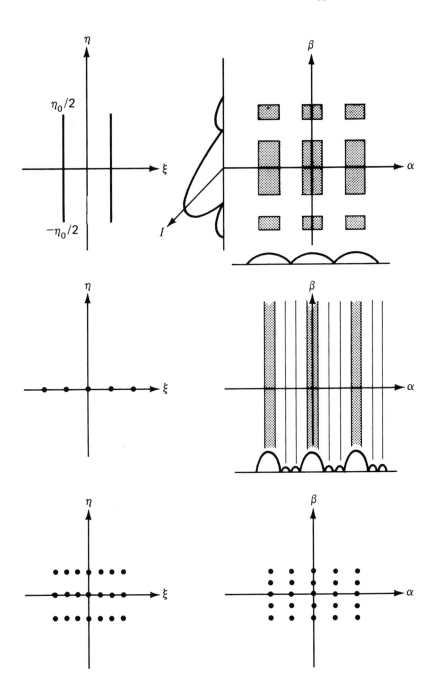

Figure 3-3. (Continued)

where $H(x)$ = Heaviside Function:

$$H(x) = \begin{cases} 0, x < 0 \\ 1, x \geq 0 \end{cases} \tag{3.15}$$

The diffraction pattern is

$$U(\alpha, \beta) = H\eta_0 \frac{\sin(k_0\beta\eta_0/2)}{(k_0\beta\eta_0/2)} \tag{3.16}$$

The limiting cases when $\eta_0 \to \infty$ and $\eta_0 \to 0$ are

$$\lim_{\eta \to \infty} \frac{\sin(k_0\beta\eta_0/2)}{(k_0\beta\eta_0/2)} = 2\pi\delta(\beta) \tag{3.17}$$

(a single line along the α axis)

and

$$\lim_{\eta \to 0} \frac{\sin(k_0\beta\eta_0/2)}{(k_0\beta\eta_0/2)} = 1 \tag{3.18}$$

(a uniform density distribution)

3. Two points spaced a distance b apart along the ξ axis and centered at the origin. The density for this distribution is

$$\rho(\xi, \eta) = \delta(\eta)[\delta(\xi + b/2) + \delta(\xi - b/2)] \tag{3.19}$$

The corresponding diffraction pattern is

$$U(\alpha, \beta) = 2H\cos(k_0 b\alpha/2) \tag{3.20}$$

This diffraction pattern appears as a series of stripes parallel to the β axis, separated by a distance equal to $(b/\lambda_0)^{-1}$.

4. Two parallel strips, each of length η_0, separated by a distance b, have a density given by

$$\rho(\xi, \eta) =$$

$$[H(\eta + \eta_0/2) - H(\eta - \eta_0/2)][\delta(\xi - b/2) + \delta(\xi + b/2)] \tag{3.21}$$

The corresponding diffraction pattern is

$$U(\alpha, \beta) = \eta_0 \frac{\sin(k_0\beta\eta_0/2)\cos(k_0\alpha b/2)}{(k_0\beta\eta_0/2)} \tag{3.22}$$

This diffraction pattern is similar to 3.20 for two points. The pattern has now become two-dimensional with stripes of decreasing density in the β direction.

5. A one-dimensional array of $2M + 1$ spots along the ξ axis separated by a distance b has a density given by

$$\rho(\xi, \eta) = \delta(\eta) \sum_{m=-M}^{M} \delta(\xi - mb) \tag{3.23}$$

The diffraction picture for 3.23 is found using the finite cosine sum. It is[a]

$$\sum_{m=0}^{M} \cos mx = \frac{1}{2} \frac{\sin Mx}{\sin(x/2)}, \quad M \gg 1 \tag{3.24}$$

The diffraction pattern corresponding to 3.22 is found using 3.23. The result is

$$U(\alpha, \beta) = H \left\{ \frac{\sin[2M(k_0 \alpha b/2)]}{\sin(k_0 \alpha b/2)} - 1 \right\} \tag{3.25}$$

The maxima of 3.25 are at

$$\alpha = 2r\pi/k_0 b = r/(b/\lambda_0), \quad r = 0, \pm 1, \pm 2, \pm 3, \dots$$

6. A two-dimensional square array of points, with spacing b along the ξ axis and spacing a along the η axis. The density is

$$\rho(\xi, \eta) = \sum_{m=0}^{M} \sum_{n=0}^{N} \delta(\xi - mb) \delta(\eta - na) \tag{3.26}$$

The diffraction pattern is

$$U(\alpha, \beta) = \frac{1}{4} H \frac{\sin[2M(k_0 b\alpha/2)]}{\sin(k_0 b\alpha/2)} \cdot \frac{\sin[2N(k_0 a\alpha/2)]}{\sin(k_0 a\alpha/2)}, \tag{3.27}$$

$$M \gg 1, N \gg 1$$

The maxima or bright spots for 3.26 occur when

$$\alpha = r/(b/\lambda_0) \tag{3.28}$$

and

$$\beta = s/(a/\lambda_0) \tag{3.29}$$

where $\quad r = 0, \pm 1, \pm 2, \pm 3, \dots$ $\qquad$ (3.30a)

and $\quad s = 0, \pm 1, \pm 2, \pm 3, \dots$ $\qquad$ (3.30b)

Note that in the preceding cases, the basic distance between spots is

[a] This formula is written for M large. The approximation used is $M \approx M - 1$, $M \gg 1$. The result for the finite sum for any M is

$$\sum_{m=0}^{M} \cos mx = \left\{ \cos \frac{mx}{2} \sin \frac{(M+1)x}{2} \right\} \Big/ \sin \frac{x}{2}$$

inversely proportional to the object distances. The general result is that large inter-object distances in the original picture correspond to small inter-spot distances in the diffraction patterns. The occurrence of distinct spots in the diffraction pattern can be interpreted as coming from objects in the original picture with a particular length. However, it is not possible geometrically to place the lengths in the original picture that gave rise to the diffraction spots. One method of experimentally placing a scale on the diffraction pattern is to diffract a lattice or grating of a known size. The spacing in the known diffraction pattern can then be compared with those in the pattern for calibration. An absolute scale can be devised from the test-grating diffraction pattern.

The Diffraction Patterns of Transmission Pictures of Helices

The study of the diffraction patterns of right circular helices with various orientations is a good example for analysis. Here is a case where much geometrical object information can be gathered by studying the diffraction pattern. The theoretical analysis serves to shed light on the location of the major parts of the diffraction pattern and their relations to the basic parameters of the object.

Consider first a helix aligned along the ζ axis of the aperture plane. The parametric equations of the helix are (refer to equation 2.34 and following):

$$\xi = a \cos \phi$$
$$\eta = a \sin \phi \qquad (3.31)$$
$$\zeta = (a \tan \alpha) \phi$$

It will be convenient to use the generalized three-dimensional form of the diffraction integral that corresponds to that given in equation 3.10. It is

$$U(\alpha, \beta, \gamma) = H \int \int \int \rho(\xi, \eta, \zeta) e^{jk_0(\alpha\xi + \beta\eta + \gamma\zeta)} \, d\xi \, d\eta \, d\zeta \qquad (3.32)$$

The diffraction pattern of a two-dimensional picture is found from 3.32 by using an appropriate density function.

The optical density of a transmission picture of a vertically aligned helix can be found from 3.31, or

$$\rho(\eta, \zeta) = \delta(\eta/a - \sin \phi)$$
$$= \delta\left(\eta/a - \sin\left(\frac{\zeta}{a \tan \alpha}\right)\right) \qquad (3.33)$$

The sinusoidal density variation of 3.33 can be substituted in 3.32 and readily integrated with respect to ζ. The remaining integral is

$$U(\beta, \gamma) = Ha \tan \alpha \int_{-\zeta}^{\zeta} e^{jk_0(\beta a \sin \bar{\zeta} + a\gamma\bar{\zeta} \tan \alpha)} \, d\bar{\zeta} \qquad (3.34)$$

where $\quad \bar{\zeta} = \zeta/(a \tan \alpha)$.

The integral 3.34 can be evaluated by using the expansion formula for an exponential trigonometric function. It is

$$e^{jk_0 \beta \sin \bar{\zeta}} = \sum_{n=-\infty}^{\infty} J_n(k_0 \beta a) \, e^{jn\bar{\zeta}} \qquad (3.35)$$

where $\quad J_n$ is the Bessel function of the first kind.

The substitution of 3.35 into 3.32 yields a result that is readily evaluated. The final infinite series expansion is

$$U(\beta, \gamma) = Ha \tan \alpha \sum_{n=-\infty}^{\infty} J_n(k_0 \beta a) \frac{\sin[\bar{\zeta}(n + k_0 a\gamma \tan \alpha)]}{(n + k_0 a\gamma \tan \alpha)} \qquad (3.36)$$

It is instructive to write out the first few terms of 3.36. They are

$$U(\beta, \gamma) = H\{J_0(k_0 \beta a) \frac{\sin \bar{\zeta}(k_0 a\gamma \tan \alpha)}{(k_0 a\gamma \tan \alpha)}$$

$$+ \; J_{\pm 1}(k_0 \beta a) \frac{\sin \bar{\zeta}(\pm 1 + k_0 a\gamma \tan \alpha)}{(\pm 1 + k_0 a\gamma \tan \alpha)}$$

$$+ \; J_{\pm 2}(k_0 \beta a) \frac{\sin \bar{\zeta}(\pm 2 + k_0 a\gamma \tan \alpha)}{(\pm 2 + k_0 a\gamma \tan \alpha)} \; + \ldots \quad (3.37)$$

The first term of 3.37 has its first maximum at the simultaneous maxima of both factors, or at $\gamma = 0$, $\beta = 0$. Other maxima occur at $\beta = 0$, $\gamma = \gamma_{mo}$, where γ_{mo} are the higher order maxima of J_0. Since the actual diffraction picture is proportional to the intensity, the first maximum will predominate. The second term of 3.37 has its major maxima at

$$\beta = \pm 1.8411/k_0 a \quad \text{and} \quad \gamma = \pm \frac{1}{k_0 a \tan \alpha} \qquad (3.38a)$$

The equations of 3.38a can be interpreted as contributing four spots in all four quadrants to the diffraction picture. The third term of 3.37 has its major maxima at

$$\beta = \pm 3.054/k_0 a, \quad \text{and} \quad \gamma = \pm \frac{2}{k_0 a \tan \alpha}, \qquad (3.38b)$$

or in general

$$\beta = \pm x_n/k_0 a, \quad \text{and} \quad \gamma = \pm \frac{n}{k_0 a \tan \alpha}, \qquad (3.38c)$$

where $\quad x_n$ is the value of x that satisfies $J_n' = 0$.

Note that the higher order major maxima move progressively[b] away from the center of the pattern at $\beta = 0$, $\gamma = 0$. The higher order Bessel functions have successively smaller major maxima. The spots then get progressively dimmer, moving away from the center of the diffraction pattern.

The preceding analysis can be used to determine the geometrical parameters of the helix. These are (1) the radius a, (2) the pitch angle α, and (3) the length of the helix d. The physical scale of the diffraction pattern must first be established with a test grating. The γ and β location of the first maximum directly gives the values of $k_0 a$ and α. The determination of the length of the helix is made by noting the distance between striations about the individual spots. The striation separation is given by finding the subsidiary maxima of the $(\sin x)/x$ pattern of 3.36, or

$$\bar{\zeta} = \frac{q\pi}{n + k_0 a\gamma \tan \alpha} \tag{3.39}$$

where $q = \pm 1, \pm 2, \pm 3, \ldots$

γ = value of the maximum location

$\bar{\zeta} = \zeta/(\alpha \tan \alpha)$

The Diffraction Pattern of a Rotated Helix

The diffraction pattern of a helix that is not perfectly aligned with the coordinate axis is considerably more complicated than that of the preceding section. The density function of a helix that is rotated about the y axis is given by 2.42 and is repeated below in slightly different form.[c]

$$\rho(\eta, \zeta) = \delta[(\zeta/a) - \tan \alpha \sin^{-1} (\eta/a) \cos \theta - \sin \theta (1 - \eta^2/a^2)^{1/2}] \tag{3.40}$$

The substitution of 3.40 into the diffraction integral produces the following result

$$U(\beta, \gamma) = Ha \int e^{jk_0 a(\zeta u \tan \alpha \, \cos \, \theta + (\eta \, \sin u - \zeta \, \sin \theta \, \cos u))} \cos u \, du \tag{3.41}$$

where $u = \sin^{-1} (\eta/a)$.

Each exponential trigonometric term of 3.41 must be expanded in an infinite series similar to 3.35. The resulting integral of 3.41 is easily evaluated. The final diffraction pattern consists of a double infinite series expansion. It is

---

[b] Note that the maxima of the Bessel functions (i.e., the x_n for which $J_n'(x_n) = 0$) are: $x_0 = 0$, $x_1 = 1.841$, $x_2 = 3.054$, $x_3 = 4.20119$, $x_4 = 5.31$, $x_5 = 6.41$, $x_6 = 7.51$, from *Handbook of Mathematical Functions*, by M. Abramowitz and I. Stegun, Dover Publications, 1965, p. 409.

[c] Note in the limiting case of $\theta \to 0$, the following results will not agree with the preceding section for $\theta = 0$ because the projection planes are different.

$$U(\beta, \gamma) = H \sum_{n=-\infty}^{\infty} J_n(k_0 a \beta) \sum_{m=-\infty}^{\infty} j^m J_m(k_0 a \zeta \sin \theta)$$

$$\times \left[\frac{\sin (\pi/2) (m + n + 1 + k_0 a \zeta \cos \theta \tan \alpha)}{(m + n + 1 + k_0 a \zeta \cos \theta \tan \alpha)} \right.$$

$$\left. + \frac{\sin (\pi/2)(m + n - 1 + k_0 a \zeta \cos \theta \tan \alpha)}{(m + n - 1 + k_0 a \zeta \cos \theta \tan \alpha)} \right] \quad (3.42)$$

An Illustrative Example, Showing the Application of Diffraction Methods to Structural Determination

Certain smooth muscle proteins are known to have the form of a striated, rather flat ribbon. The striations appear as stripes perpendicular to the long axis of the ribbon. In practice, the muscle proteins in the electron micrographs appear twisted or bent. The basic problem will be to characterize the structure from available transmission pictures of a flattened and a twisted, bent ribbon.[d] It is also known that the thickness of the ribbon is negligible, and that the axis of the ribbon lies in the plane of observation. Two simplified models of the ribbon are shown in Figures 3-4 and 3-5. The actual models were made from black tape that was placed on a glass microscope slide. The glass slide was then placed in the object plane of the Fourier analyzer (i.e., diffractometer) shown in Figure 3-6. The Fourier transform (i.e., Frauenhoffer diffraction pattern) of the object was photographed at the focal plane of the lens. The system was calibrated using a Ronchi grating, which consisted of a series of parallel lines with a spacing corresponding to 50 lines per inch (about 2 lines/mm). The optical density on the grating is represented by (refer to equations 3.14 and 3.23):

$$\rho(\xi, \eta) = \lim_{\eta_0 \to \infty} [H(\eta + \eta_0/2) - H(\eta - \eta_0/2)] \cdot \sum_{m=-M}^{M} \delta(\xi - mb) \quad (3.43)$$

The diffraction picture corresponding to 3.43 is found using the diffraction integral 3.10 (see equations 3.17 and 3.25). The result is

$$U(\alpha, \beta) = 2\pi H \, \delta(\beta) \left\{ \frac{\sin [2M(k_0 \alpha b/2)]}{\sin (k_0 \alpha b/2)} - 1 \right\} \quad (3.44)$$

The picture corresponding to 3.44 represents a series of bright spots along the α axis of the diffraction plane. The spots are shown in Figure 3-7. Note that there is a circular pattern around each spot that is due to the finite size of the point source in the collimator of the Fourier analyzer. The maxima of 3.44 occur at

$$\alpha = x/r = 2i\pi/k_0 b = i/(b/\lambda_0), \quad i = 0, \pm 1, \pm 2, \pm 3, \ldots \quad (3.45)$$

[d]The results given in this section are due to Leslie Brown.

Figure 3-4. Flattened Ribbon

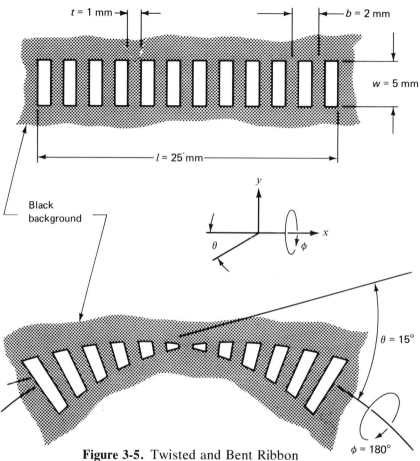

Figure 3-5. Twisted and Bent Ribbon

The focal length of the lens, r, can be calculated by measuring the separation between maxima on the diffraction picture (i.e., $x = \delta_{cal} = 7.5$ mm). The focal length r is then

$$r = \left(\frac{b}{\lambda_0}\right)x = \left(\frac{b}{\lambda_0}\right)\delta_{cal} = \frac{0.5 \text{ mm/line}}{0.63 \times 10^{-3}\text{mm}} \cdot 7.5 \text{ mm} = 5950 \text{ mm} \qquad (3.46)$$

The two-dimensional density distribution for the flat ribbon consists of two terms. The first represents a rectangular opening of length l and width w. The second represents N stripes of height w and t, spaced a center-to-center distance of s apart. This density distribution is

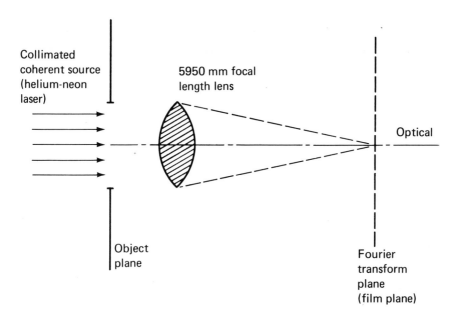

Figure 3-6. Optical Fourier Analyzer Set-up

$$\rho(\xi, \eta) = [H(\xi - l/2) - H(\xi + l/2)][H(\eta - w/2) - H(\eta + w/2)]$$

$$- [H(\eta - w/2) - H(\eta + w/2)] \sum_m \{H[\xi - m(t/2 - s)]$$

$$- H[\xi + m(t/2 + s)]\} \quad (3.47)$$

The two-dimensional diffraction pattern corresponding to 3.47 is given by

$$U(\alpha, \beta) = H \frac{\sin(k_0 \beta w/2)}{(k_0 \beta w/2)}$$

$$\times \left[\frac{\sin(k_0 \alpha l/2)}{(k_0 \alpha l/2)} - \frac{\sin(\alpha t/2) \sin(k_0 M \alpha s/2)}{(\alpha t/2) \sin(k_0 \alpha s/2)} \right] \quad (3.48)$$

where M = total number of stripes.

There are a number of characteristic periodicities associated with 3.48 which appear as bright striations in the diffraction picture. The vertical striations (β direction) occur when

$$k_0 \beta w/2 = n\pi, \quad n = 0, \pm 1, \pm 2, \ldots \quad (3.49a)$$

or when

$$\beta = (y/r) = n/(w/\lambda_0), \quad n = 0, \pm 1, \pm 2, \ldots \quad (3.49b)$$

Photograph by Leslie Brown.

Figure 3-7. Diffraction Pattern of Ronchi Ruling

Measurements of the diffraction pattern give a separation between vertical striations of $y = 0.75$ mm. The ribbon width w is then found, using 3.49 with 3.46, or

$$w = \frac{r\lambda_0}{y} = \frac{5.95 \text{ mm} \times 0.63 \text{ mm} \times 10^{-3}}{0.75 \text{ mm}} = 5 \text{ mm} \qquad (3.50)$$

The striations that are closest together in the x direction correspond to the largest dimension in the ribbon (i.e., the length l). The striations with the largest separation along the x axis correspond to the stripe width w. The striations having a separation intermediate between smallest and largest correspond to the stripe separation s. The diffraction picture for the ribbon is shown in Figure 3-8.

A drawing showing the ribbon twisted about its long axis is shown in Figure 3-9. The ribbon was bent into a V shape by moving each half down by an angle of 15° from its normal position. The effect of rotations on the original density can be seen easily by placing the transform integral in polar form. In polar coordinates, the transform integral is

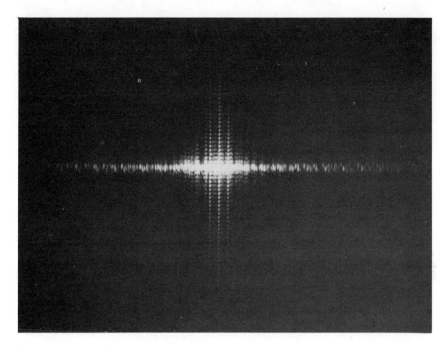

Photograph by Leslie Brown.

Figure 3-8. Diffraction Pattern for Ribbon

$$U(\rho, \phi) = H \int \int \rho(r, \theta) \, e^{jk_0 r\rho \cos(\theta - \phi)} \, \rho \, d\rho \, d\phi \qquad (3.51)$$

where
$$\xi = r \cos \theta \qquad \alpha = \rho \cos \phi$$
$$\eta = r \sin \theta \qquad \beta = \rho \sin \phi \qquad (3.52)$$

(real space)   (diffraction space)

Note that when the original density is rotated by an angle of θ_r, the argument of the cosine in the exponential of 3.51 is

$$\theta + \theta_r - \phi = \theta - (\phi - \theta_r) \qquad (3.53)$$

The effect of rotating a density by an angle θ_r in real space corresponds to rotating the corresponding diffraction pattern by $-\theta_r$. Figure 3-10 shows that the angle between the diffraction patterns for each half ribbon is equal to the real space rotation angle (or 15° in this case).

To obtain a projection of a continuous helix, a model, shown in Figure 3-11, was constructed of wire and then diffracted in the same manner as the preceding ribbon model. Its diffraction pattern is shown in Figure 3-12. The

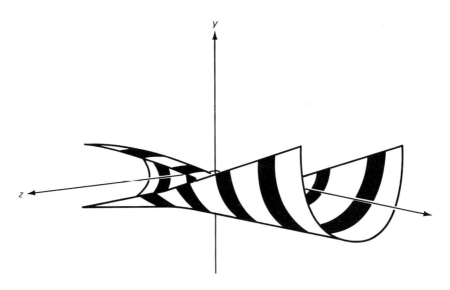

Based on original drawing by Arthur Singer.

Figure 3-9. Twisted Ribbon

low angle (i.e., nearly horizontal angle) radial lines are an artifact introduced by the iris of the diffractometer. The horizontal lines in Figure 3-12 are called layer lines and correspond to the $n = 0, \pm 1, \pm 2, \ldots$ values of the diffraction pattern (refer to equation 3.36 et seq.). The major maxima of the diffraction pattern of a helix are along an X shaped axis, about 15 degrees apart, centered about the vertical axis of Figure 3-12. The coordinates of the spot that corresponds to $n = 4$ along one of the X lines are

$$y = 1.5 \times 10^{-3} \text{ meters (horizontal coordinate)}$$

$$z = 8 \times 10^{-3} \text{ meters (vertical coordinate)}$$

(3.54)

This spot was chosen because it is the first spot that is clear of the bright center section of the diffraction pattern. The values of the helix radius a and the pitch angle α are easily found from 3.39. They are

$$a = \frac{x\lambda_0}{2\pi} \cdot \frac{r}{y} = \frac{5.31}{2\pi} \cdot 0.63 \times 10^{-6} \cdot \frac{5.95}{1.5 \times 10^{-3}} = 2.13 \times 10^{-3} \text{m}$$

$$\alpha = \tan^{-1}\left(\frac{n\lambda_0 r}{2\pi a z}\right) = \tan^{-1}\left[\frac{2 \cdot 0.63 \times 10^{-6} \cdot 5.95}{\pi \cdot 2.13 \times 10^{-3} \cdot 0.8 \times 10^{-2}}\right]$$

(3.55)

$$= \tan^{-1}(0.14) = 8°$$

Photograph by Leslie Brown.

Figure 3-10. Diffraction Pattern of Twisted Ribbon

The above results compare favorably with the actual values of $a = 2.5 \times 10^{-3}$ m and $\alpha = 6°$. Two other diffraction pictures are shown in Figures 3-13 and 3-14. Here, atoms are represented by discrete spots along a helical backbone.

Fourier Reconstruction

A Fourier reconstruction may or may not be an indirect method. It really depends on the form in which the data for reconstruction are taken. For example, the determination of crystalline structures is usually done by means of X-ray diffraction techniques. The data here occur in diffraction or transform space. A columnated beam of X-rays is directed on a crystalline sample wherein the atoms are arranged in an ordered way. This ordering results from a particular periodicity in the atomic arrangement. The X-rays

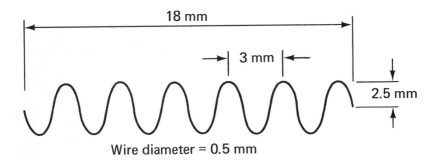

18 mm

3 mm

2.5 mm

Wire diameter = 0.5 mm

Figure 3-11. Coiled Wire Model

Photograph by Leslie Brown.

Figure 3-12. Diffraction Pattern of Coiled Wire Model

are diffracted from this regular arrangement onto a photographic film or an X-ray detector tube. The diffraction spots occur at particular places in a hemispherical region. A special arrangement is required to ensure that all the diffraction spots are recorded for subsequent reconstruction. The whole process is very time consuming, but has been found very amenable to automation. The most important point, however, is that the complete diffraction pattern is related through a Fourier transformation to the atomic structure of the crystal.

The use of a Fourier reconstruction on an object for which data are available in real space is considered to be an indirect method. Objects which occur on electron micrographs or on seismographs are reconstructed beginning with real-space information. A Fourier reconstruction for these cases is considered indirect since the process involves Fourier transforming the pictures, reconstructing in transform space, and then transforming the result back to real space.

The methods used for three-dimensional reconstruction using Fourier methods have their beginnings in crystallography. The extension of crystallographic techniques to reconstruction from two-dimensional transmission photographs is due mainly to the work of Aaron Klug and his associates at the Medical Research Council Laboratory for Molecular Biology in Cambridge, England. A good list of references for this work can be found in a paper by Mersereau and Oppenheim [5]. Much of the basis for the reconstruction work of the Klug group can be found in the papers of DeRosier and Klug [4] and that of Crowther, DeRosier, and Klug [3].

Some of the ideas fundamental to the Fourier-reconstruction techniques will be described beginning with the basic three-dimensional diffraction integral for $U(\alpha, \beta, \gamma)$. It is

$$U(\alpha, \beta, \gamma) = H \int \int \int \rho(\xi, \eta, \zeta) e^{jk_0(\alpha\xi + \beta\eta + \gamma\zeta)} \, d\xi \, d\eta \, d\zeta \qquad (3.56)$$

The three-dimensional density function appears in equation 3.56 as $\rho(\xi, \eta, \zeta)$, where ξ, η, and ζ are the orthogonal coordinates associated with ρ. The direction cosine coordinates associated with diffraction or Fourier space are α, β, and γ. The inversion of 3.56 can be accomplished by first examining the inversion of the one-dimensional form and extending the result to three dimensions. The one-dimensional diffraction integral $U(\alpha)$ is

$$U(\alpha) = H \int_{-\infty}^{\infty} \rho(u) \, e^{jk_0\alpha u} \, du \qquad (3.57)$$

The integral range in 3.57 is chosen to include all of transform space. Both sides of 3.57 are then multiplied by $e^{-jk_0\alpha\xi}$ and integrated over the infinite range.

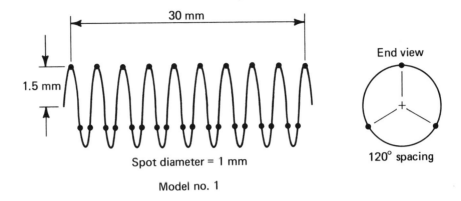

30 mm

1.5 mm

Spot diameter = 1 mm

Model no. 1

End view

120° spacing

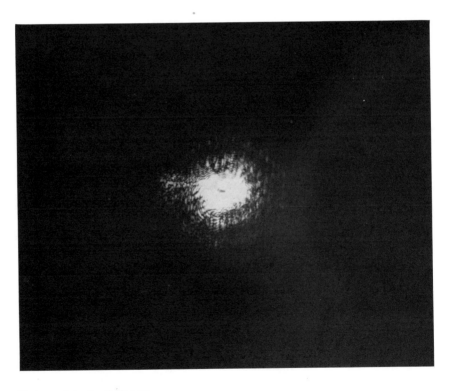

Photograph by Leslie Brown.

Figure 3-13. Helical Model No. 1 and Its Diffraction Pattern

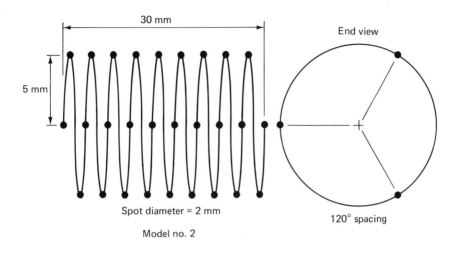

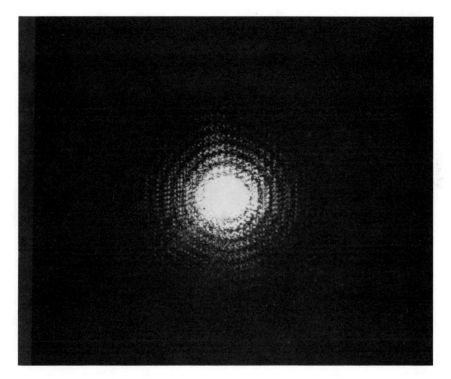

Photograph by Leslie Brown.

Figure 3-14. Helical Model No. 2 and Its Diffraction Pattern

$$\int_{-\infty}^{\infty} U(\alpha)e^{-jk_0\alpha\xi}\,d\alpha = H\int_{-\infty}^{\infty}\left[\int_{-\infty}^{\infty}\rho(u)e^{jk_0\alpha u}\,du\right]e^{-jk_0\alpha\xi}\,d\alpha \qquad (3.58)$$

A reversal in the order of integration on the right hand side of 3.58 gives the following results:

$$\int_{-\infty}^{\infty} U(\alpha)e^{-jk_0\alpha\xi}\,d\alpha = H\int_{-\infty}^{\infty}\left[\int_{-\infty}^{\infty}e^{jk_0\alpha(u-\xi)}\,d\alpha\right]\rho(u)\,du \qquad (3.59)$$

The integral in the brackets of 3.59 is an integral representation of the delta function. The basic integral for $\delta(x)$ is given by

$$\delta(x) = \frac{1}{2\pi}\int_{-\infty}^{\infty}e^{-jvx}\,dv \qquad (3.60)$$

. If the variable x in 3.60 is associated with $(u - \xi)$ of 3.59, then the density integral is easily evaluated as follows:

$$H\int_{-\infty}^{\infty}\rho(u)\left[\int_{-\infty}^{\infty}e^{jk_0\alpha(u-\xi)}\,d\alpha\right]du = 2\pi H\int_{-\infty}^{\infty}\rho(u)\,\delta(u-\xi)\,du = 2\pi H\rho(\xi) \quad (3.61)$$

The final explicit result for $\rho(\xi)$ is

$$\rho(\xi) = \frac{1}{2\pi H}\int_{-\infty}^{\infty}U(\alpha)e^{-jk_0\alpha\xi}\,d\alpha \qquad (3.62)$$

The one-dimensional result of 3.62 is extendible to three dimensions yielding

$$\rho(\xi,\,\eta,\,\zeta) = \frac{1}{(2\pi)^3 H}\int_{-\infty}^{\infty}\int\int U(\alpha,\,\beta,\,\gamma)\,e^{-jk_0(\alpha\xi+\beta\eta+\gamma\zeta)}\,d\alpha\,d\beta\,d\gamma \qquad (3.63)$$

The formal result of 3.63 for ρ allows the three-dimensional object density to be recovered from the complete three-dimensional diffraction pattern U. In practice, only a portion of the complete diffraction pattern is usually available. Furthermore, in the case of transmission pictures the diffraction pattern that is available is the transform of the projection picture. For example, consider the projection along the ξ axis, $\rho(\eta,\,\zeta)$ of the density $\rho(\xi,\,\eta,\,\zeta)$. It is given by

$$\rho(\eta,\,\zeta) = \int \rho(\xi,\,\eta,\,\zeta)\,d\xi \qquad (3.64)$$

The diffraction pattern of 3.64 is

$$U(\beta,\,\gamma) = H\int\int\left[\int \rho(\xi,\,\eta,\,\zeta)\,d\xi\right]e^{jk_0(\beta\eta+\gamma\zeta)}\,d\eta\,d\zeta \qquad (3.65)$$

Note that the value of U given in 3.65 corresponds to the general diffraction integral representation of 3.56 evaluated at $\alpha = 0$. Stated in another way, the diffraction pattern of the projection 3.64 is identical to a slice of transform space in the same orientation as the original projection. The above result can be extended to three dimensions and is called the projection theorem [3]. A two-dimensional form of the projection theorem can be proved by beginning with the projection integral, which includes a rotation angle ψ. Equation 2.9 shows that

$$\int_{S_0}^{S_f} \rho(x, y)\, ds = \int_{S_0}^{S_f} \rho\left(x,\ x\tan\psi + \frac{\eta}{\cos\psi}\right) \sec\psi\, dx = P(\eta) \quad (3.66)$$

The geometry for 3.66 is shown in Figure 2-5. The differential ds is along the projection lines and ψ is the angle with the x axis. Equation 3.66 can be substituted into 3.65 by associating $P(\eta)$ with the integral in the brackets. The result is

$$U(\beta, \gamma) = H \int\int \int \rho(\xi,\ \xi\tan\psi + \bar{\eta})\, d\xi \cdot e^{jk_0[\xi(\alpha + \beta\tan\psi) + \bar{\eta}\beta + \gamma]}\, d\bar{\eta}\, d\zeta \quad (3.67)$$

where $\qquad \bar{\eta} = \eta/\cos\psi$

$$\xi(\alpha + \beta\tan\psi) + \eta\beta + \gamma\zeta = \alpha\xi + (\xi\tan\psi + \bar{\eta})\beta + \gamma\zeta.$$

When the coefficient of ξ in the exponent of equation 3.67 is set equal to zero, then it reduces to

$$U(\beta, \gamma) = H \int\int \left[\int \rho(\xi,\ \xi\tan\psi + \bar{\eta})\, d\xi\right] e^{jk_0(\beta\eta + \gamma\zeta)}\, d\eta\, d\zeta \quad (3.68)$$

Thus the pattern 3.68 is equivalent to a slice of diffraction space given by

$$\alpha + \beta\tan\psi = 0 \qquad \text{or} \qquad \beta = -\alpha\cot\psi \quad (3.69)$$

Equation 3.69 shows that the slice in diffraction space is in the same direction as the projection.

The numerical inversion of the Fourier transform integral requires a discrete form for the integral. The rectangular integration form for ρ is

$$\rho(\xi, \eta, \zeta) = \frac{1}{(2\pi)^3 H} \Delta\alpha\, \Delta\beta\, \Delta\gamma \sum_{i,k,l} U(\alpha_i, \beta_k, \gamma_l)\, e^{-jk_0(\alpha_i\xi + \beta_k\eta + \gamma_l\zeta)} \quad (3.70)$$

The summation in 3.70 requires that the intervals be evenly spaced along the α, β, and γ directions. Thus it is required that

$$\alpha_i = ia$$
$$\beta_k = kb \quad (3.71)$$
and
$$\gamma_l = lc$$

where a, b, and c are proportional to the distances between sample points in the α, β, and γ directions. The integral representation for ρ is also dependent on a unique representation for U in terms of its discrete values. This problem is well known to electrical engineers in terms of the sampling function representation of a function [6]. The uniqueness involves a band limiting requirement on the transform variables α, β, and γ. The one-dimensional integral illustrates some of the problems involved in inverting the transform. The discrete and continuous forms $\rho(\xi)$ are

$$\rho(\xi) \;=\; \frac{1}{2H} \int U(\alpha) e^{-jk_0 \alpha \xi}\, d\alpha \;\simeq\; \frac{\Delta\alpha}{2\pi} \sum_i U(ia) e^{jk_0 \xi(ia)} \qquad (3.72)$$

A little reflection is now required before the actual operations in 3.72 can be carried out. The number of summation points and their spacing a must be determined in a consistent way. The practical reconstruction problem concerns an object of finite extent that contains details of a certain size, say l_0. The sample size used on a real space picture of the object must sample at points that are l_0 apart or less. The transform of the object picture would then contain the information needed to reproduce the original object after an inverse transformation. The entire process must be consistent. The bandwidth must be sufficient to accommodate a real space sampling that reflects the actual functional variations. The problem is analogous to the approximation of a function by a Fourier series. The highest harmonic used in a functional approximation is chosen so as to reproduce the original function to some desired accuracy. The requirements of this process can be prescribed precisely if the Fourier transform of the object is available.

One prescription for resolution in reconstruction can be found from the sampling theorem. The sampling theorem can be used to describe a real space representation for $\rho(\xi)$ in terms of its samples or to represent a Fourier space transform $U(\alpha)$. Consider first a density distribution $\rho(\xi)$ which has a Fourier transform that is zero for $|\alpha| > \alpha_m$. This property serves to limit the Fourier transform of the object. The density $\rho(\xi)$ is then given uniquely by

$$\rho(\xi) \;=\; \sum_{i=-\infty}^{\infty} \rho\!\left(\frac{i}{2\alpha_m}\right) \frac{\sin(k_0 \alpha_m \xi - i\pi)}{(k_0 \alpha_m - i\pi)} \qquad (3.73)$$

Notice that the samples in 3.73 are located $1/2\alpha_m$ apart. As an example consider an object with its fine detail spaced a distance ξ_0 apart. The required bandwidth is $4\pi\alpha_m$ where α_m is given by the solution of

$$\xi_0 \;=\; \frac{1}{2k_0 \alpha_m} \qquad (3.74a)$$

or

$$\alpha_m \;=\; \frac{1}{2k_0 \xi_0} \qquad (3.74b)$$

A real object produces a transform that is infinite in extent. The truncation required by limiting the bandwidth is a source of error involved in the reconstruction technique. Pictures with sharp edges produce transforms that are by no means band limited. It then becomes necessary to "round" the edges artificially to bound a sufficient portion of the transform within the band limited range.

The sampling representation of the diffraction pattern $U(\alpha)$ is similar to 3.74. It involves a transform of $U(\alpha)$ (i.e., $\rho(\xi)$) that is *space* limited to $|\xi| \leq \xi_m$. Here $2\xi_m$ is the maximum extent of the object. A unique representation of $U(\alpha)$ by the sampling theorem is

$$U(\alpha) = \sum_{i=-\infty}^{\infty} U\left(\frac{i\pi}{\xi_m}\right) \frac{\sin(k_0 \alpha \xi_m - i\pi)}{(k_0 \alpha \xi_m - i\pi)} \tag{3.75}$$

The sampling representation in 3.75 can also be used as an interpolation function. This interpolation is needed for actual data since the finite formula 3.70 requires that the sample points be presented on a regular lattice. The actual data points, say for $U(\alpha)$, can be interpolated onto a regular lattice $U(\bar{\alpha})$ by the relation

$$U(\bar{\alpha}) = \sum_{i} U(\alpha_i) \frac{\sin \pi(\bar{\alpha} - \alpha_i)}{\pi(\bar{\alpha} - \alpha_i)} \tag{3.76}$$

A three-dimensional interpolation function is similar to 3.76 and appears as a product of three separable $(\sin x)/x$ functions. It is

$$U(\bar{\alpha}, \bar{\beta}, \bar{\gamma}) = \sum_{i,j,l} U(\alpha_i, \beta_j, \gamma_l) \frac{\sin \pi(\bar{\alpha} - \alpha_i)}{\pi(\bar{\alpha} - \alpha_i)}$$
$$\cdot \frac{\sin \pi(\bar{\beta} - \beta_j)}{\pi(\bar{\beta} - \beta_j)} \cdot \frac{\sin \pi(\bar{\gamma} - \gamma_l)}{\pi(\bar{\gamma} - \gamma_l)} \tag{3.77}$$

The summation indices of 3.77 are chosen to include a sufficient number of points for a desired degree of accuracy. Actual practice involves an under or over supply of data points. A very efficient way of using available data points has been given by Crowther et al [3]. A least-square matrix approximation is used to reduce the data to the desired lattice.

References

1. Born, M., and Wolfe, E. *Principles of Optics*, 3d. ed. London: Pergamon Press, 1965.

2. Brown, E.B. *Modern Optics*. London: Reinhold Publishing Co., Chapman and Hall, 1965.

3. Crowther, R.A., DeRosier, D.J., and Klug, A. "The Reconstruction of Three-dimensional Structures from Projections and Its Application to Electron Microscopy." *Proceedings of the Royal Society*, London, Series A., vol. 317 (1970), pp. 319-340.

4. DeRosier, D.J., and Klug, A. "Reconstruction of Three-dimensional Structures from Electron Micrographs." *Nature*, vol. 217 (1968), pp. 130-134.

5. Mersereau, R.M., and Oppenheim, A.V. "Digital Reconstruction of Multi-dimensional Signals from Their Projection." *Proceedings of the I.E.E.E.*, vol. 62, no. 10 (1974), pp. 1319-1338.

6. Shannon, C.E. "Communication in the Presence of Noise." *Proceedings of the I.R.E.*, vol. 37, no. 10 (1949), pp. 10-21.

4 Direct Methods of Reconstruction

The preceding chapter was concerned with a particular type of structural analysis of photographs. When the original data appear on a photograph, the techniques of chapter 3 are characterized as indirect methods. The determination of structural information *directly* from a photograph is characterized as a direct method. It is possible in certain special cases to produce an identical result using either a direct or an indirect method. In most cases, the question is not so much which method is better, but rather, which yields an answer that is closer to reality. Even this concept may be questioned since, to paraphrase an old adage, the reality is in the eyes of the beholder. The reason why the reconstruction problem is so difficult is that the unknown is the object, and the information about the object is obtained only through projections in real space or transforms in Fourier space. The nature of the method used to produce structural information depends in part on the nature of the biological object. This chapter is concerned with giving a number of different methods for determining structure directly from photographs. The treatment is not meant to be exhaustive. Rather, the intent is to get the reader started in thinking about possible ways of attacking particular problems. Many times there is insufficient information available for reconstruction or for characterizing the object in some structural way. The major objective then is to do the best possible job with the available information.

The Determination of Basic Structural Lengths

The analysis of biological pictures for structural information can proceed by finding the basic lengths or shapes that occur. The simplest way to determine lengths in a picture is to measure them. This procedure is not as straightforward as it seems. The viewer must not only contend with the fuzziness of the object, but also with the problem of the overlapping of more than one object at a time. The object may also be tilted inward from the photograph. The true geometrical length is then masked in the projection picture. The determination of length by computers does not proceed in the same manner as that used by a human observer. Mathematical algorithms must be developed to locate the object and find its shape or length.

A very simple example is shown in Figure 4-1. A line segment of length l

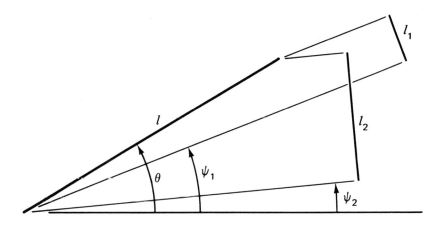

Figure 4-1. Two Projections of a Line of Length l

is tilted at an angle θ with respect to the x axis. The problem is to determine the length of the segment automatically. The entire picture plane could be searched element by element for the object, but this process is time-consuming. An alternative method is to look at the projections of the object. This projection is actually the projection of a projection if the object is seen in transmission. The length of the projection in two angular views corresponding to tilt angles ψ_1 and ψ_2 is given by l_1 and l_2 where

$$l_1 = l \sin (\theta - \psi_1) \tag{4.1a}$$

$$l_2 = l \sin (\theta - \psi_2) \tag{4.1b}$$

Equations 4.1 can be solved simultaneously for θ, the inclination angle to the picture plane, and l, the true length. The result is

$$\theta = \sin^{-1}\left\{ \frac{\sin \psi_1 - \bar{l} \sin \psi_2}{1 + \bar{l}^2 - 2 \cos (\psi_1 - \psi_2)} \right\}$$

and

$$l = l_1/\sin (\theta - \psi) \tag{4.2}$$

where

$$\bar{l} = l_1/l_2$$

This result can also be used to locate the line segment in the x-y plane of the picture. The success of this method of determining the length depends on knowing a priori the shape of the object in the picture. In addition, the object must be known to have the only nonzero optical densities in the picture. A practical case would have to include the effect of background densities and shape distortions in the picture in the determination of actual shape and position.

Finding the Parameters of a Helix

The previous chapter on diffraction methods showed that the basic lengths or dimensions of a picture can be observed in the transform plane. Similar, but not identical, picture operations can be performed in real space. As an example, consider the problem of finding the parameters of a helix (refer to equation 3.38 et seq.). One real space method consists of overlaying two transparencies of the picture, as shown in Figure 4-2. The two transparencies are moved with respect to each other. A stationary light spot is made to penetrate both pictures. The integrated result is known mathematically as the auto-correlation function. The two-dimensional auto-correlation function $\rho_{11}(\tau_1, \tau_2)$, corresponding to an optical projection $P(x, y)$, is

$$\rho_{11}(\tau_1, \tau_2) = \int_0^{y_1} \int_0^{x_1} P(x, y) P(x - \tau_1, y - \tau_2) \, dx \, dy \qquad (4.3)$$

where x_1 is the x correlation interval

  y_1 is the y correlation interval

Equation 4.3 can be used to find the parameters of the helix. Usually one cannot measure the parameters directly because of the low quality of the image. The pictures of the helix are overlapped and moved longitudinally with respect to each other. Using the parametric equations for a helix for the optical projection $P(x, y)$, the one-dimensional auto-correlation function $\rho_{11}(\tau_1)$ is

$$\rho_{11}(\tau_1) = \int_0^{x_1} a^2 \sin\left(\frac{z}{c}\right) \sin\left(\frac{z - \tau_1}{c}\right) dz \qquad (4.4)$$

where $a \sin (z/c)$ is the helical projection

  a = radius of the helix

  $c = a \tan \alpha$

  α = pitch angle of the helix

The integrated value of 4.4 is

$$\rho_{11}(\tau_1) = a^2 \left\{ \cos\left(\frac{\tau_1}{c}\right)\left[\frac{x_1}{2} - \frac{1}{4} \sin\left(2\frac{x_1}{c}\right)\right] \right.$$
$$\left. + \frac{1}{4} \sin\left(\frac{\tau_1}{c}\right)\left[1 - \cos\left(2\frac{x_1}{c}\right)\right] \right\} \qquad (4.5)$$

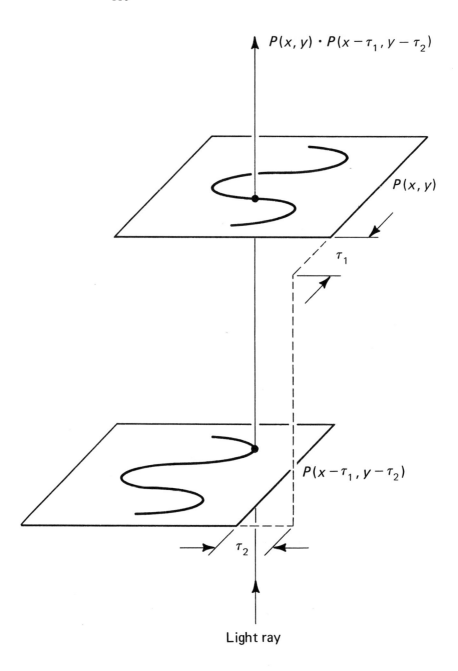

Figure 4-2. A Pictorial Interpretation of Convolution

If the correlation interval x_1 is large compared with one, then the auto-correlation function reduces to

$$\rho_{11}(\tau_1) \simeq a^2 \cos{(\tau_1/c)}, \qquad x_1 \gg 1 \qquad (4.6)$$

A display of ρ_{11} given by 4.6 would show a maximum of a^2 when $\tau_1 = c$, or

$$\rho_{11}(\tau_1) = a^2, \qquad \tau_1 = c \qquad (4.7)$$

The values of the helix radius a and the pitch angle α can be found directly from 4.7. The advantage of using the foregoing procedure for determining the parameters of a helix is that the optical picture noise due to artifacts and specimen preparation is relatively uncorrelated and does not contribute appreciably to ρ_{11}. The parameters of a helix can also be determined directly from the projection photograph.

Direct Determination of Periodicity

The method presented here[a] can be used for a wide class of objects which are considered to be periodic. Figure 4-3 shows a strip of width $2l$ in which it is required to find the periodicity along the longitudinal or x axis. The undulation can be considered as the projection of a helix or a simple model for a more complicated structure. The projection of the photograph is shown diagrammatically in Figure 4-4. The picture is represented by an optical density $P(x, y)$. The basic projection integral for the projection $\bar{P}$ is

$$\int P(x, y) \, d\xi = \bar{P} \qquad (4.8)$$

The equation for a projection line is

$$y = x \tan{\psi} + \eta/\cos{\psi}. \qquad (4.9)$$

where

$$\psi = \text{tilt angle}$$

The incremental distance $d\xi$ along the projection line is

$$d\xi = dx \sqrt{1 + (dy/dx)^2} = \sec{\psi} \, dx \qquad (4.10)$$

The final value of the projection integral is obtained by substituting equations 4.10 and 4.9 in 4.8 with the result

$$\int P(x, x \tan{\psi} + \eta/\cos{\psi}) \sec{\psi} \, dx = \bar{P}(\eta) \qquad (4.11)$$

---

[a] This section was prepared in collaboration with K.U. Sivaprasad.

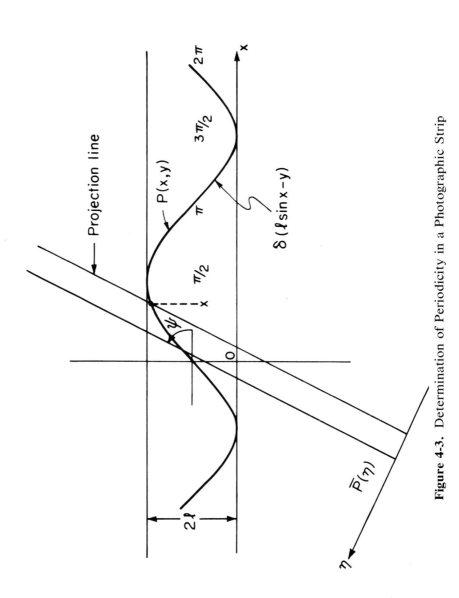

Figure 4-3. Determination of Periodicity in a Photographic Strip

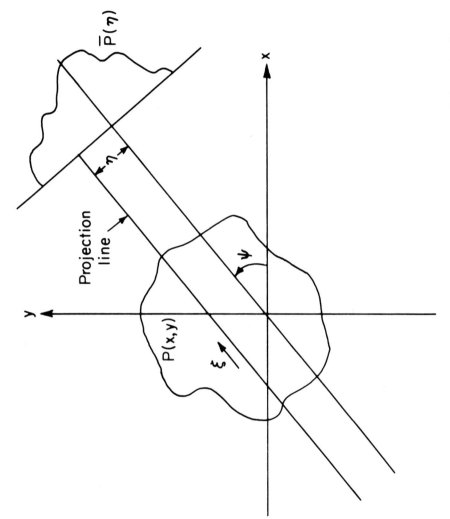

Figure 4-4. Diagram of the Projection of a Photograph at an Oblique Angle ψ

where P is the projection object on the photograph, and

$\overline{P}$ is the angular projection of P

A sinusoidal curve $P(x, y)$ is represented by the following line density

$$P(x, y) = \delta(l \sin x - y) \qquad (4.12)$$

The projection value $\overline{P}(\eta)$ is found by substituting equation 4.12 into 4.11 or

$$\sec \psi \int \delta (l \sin x - x \tan \psi - \eta/\cos \psi) \, dx = \overline{P}(\eta) \qquad (4.13)$$

It is instructive to consider the region where the argument of the delta function in 4.13 is zero. This region is given by

$$\eta = l \cos \psi \sin x - x \sin \psi, \qquad (4.14)$$

or

$$\eta/\sin \psi = (l \cot \psi) \sin x - x, \qquad \psi \neq 0 \qquad (4.15)$$

It is apparent from Figure 4-3 that when the projection line is tangent to the sine curve at $x = 0$, the projection $\overline{P}$ will have a local maximum. The local maximum of $\overline{P}$ will occur again a full cycle later. At other places along $\overline{P}$ or at other values of the slope angle ψ, no such local maxima exist. A plot of equation 4.15, in Figure 4-5, shows that only when $(l \cot \psi)$ equals one does there exist a flat region for which the projection $\overline{P}$ will have a major contribution.

The preceding method has been applied by Sandler [9] to a determination of the apparent periodicity of the collagen fibrils in a lamella of the human cornea. A large section of a lamella is shown in Figure 4-6. The fibrils are known to be roughly parallel in a single lamella. The section prepared for electron microscopy is known to be about two fibrils thick. The adjacent lamellas in the figure are roughly at right angles to the center section. The densitometered image was searched at different rotation angles.

The electron micrograph projections have been densitized using a densitometer and the output is given in Figure 4-7. Note that the number 256 is black, while 0 represents white. The numbers 59 and 58 in the figure represent the dirt spot in the photograph, which has been taken as a reference point. The horizontal length scale is half as long as the vertical scale of the printout.

The printout is used to get the one-dimensional density distribution. Four typical angles are chosen. For each angle several equidistant rays are drawn. The total density on each ray is summed, and a normalized distribution is obtained by dividing the total by the length of the ray. Linear interpolation of densities is used for the regions in which the rays do not

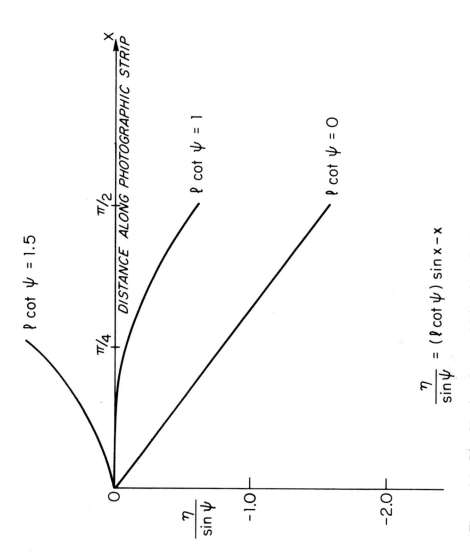

$$\frac{\eta}{\sin \psi} = (\ell \cot \psi) \sin x - x$$

Figure 4-5. Plot Used to Locate Major Contributions to Projection of a Sine Wave

115

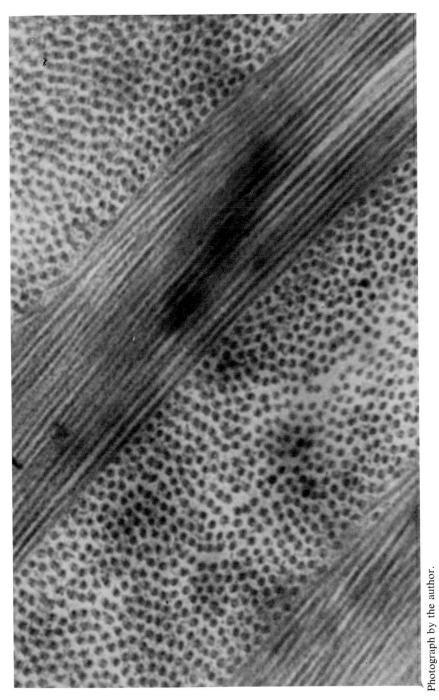

Photograph by the author.

Figure 4-6. A Posterior Section of a Lamella of the Human Cornea

127	129	125	149	118	139	120	125	131	113	126	125	109	125	123	125	117	119	131	125	127	134	113	129	174
117	121	125	137	155	138	125	145	126	127	127	123	114	111	99	107	106	109	129	129	125	133	141	125	133
141	135	156	149	153	135	135	123	127	119	115	100	91	96	101	102	109	111	115	117	113	123	129	135	153
123	121	125	123	115	130	119	115	99	103	105	99	101	95	101	109	113	111	104	113	111	113	111	133	133
125	113	115	112	123	125	115	101	112	105	93	85	99	103	109	110	109	117	117	125	120	117	129	133	133
113	121	121	119	134	123	121	123	117	103	95	83	85	89	93	97	99	101	109	115	127	129	149	151	151
131	129	132	135	137	131	122	119	137	125	113	111	115	122	123	109	106	113	119	129	126	127	137	137	151
127	131	129	132	138	139	125	121	114	124	111	119	113	119	122	133	141	143	143	147	147	143	155	145	148
144	146	132	135	137	139	121	125	119	122	121	121	129	121	137	141	137	133	124	125	134	133	138	126	125
122	130	131	127	124	121	59	119	116	118	115	115	113	113	112	110	126	121	130	138	141	148	145	135	133
109	112	115	111	106	113	58	113	122	119	121	122	111	97	91	114	117	121	119	123	133	143	141	143	135
137	131	141	130	134	129	113	139	135	135	144	129	115	97	73	109	113	109	122	119	119	126	115	111	99
123	115	113	124	127	131	123	126	137	135	117	121	101	95	93	122	127	122	133	115	123	129	117	109	109
136	126	107	111	111	119	111	127	109	109	103	95	93	90	89	111	105	109	113	113	125	136	130	126	121
119	135	131	124	107	114	119	113	102	107	93	91	81	93	91	93	95	105	101	99	101	113	109	116	108
121	127	127	135	125	141	93	143	113	121	103	99	89	81	77	83	79	82	77	69	86	90	85	98	95
123	136	109	95	111	117	139	142	125	125	125	117	111	99	87	83	79	73	75	74	86	85	83	89	93
130	129	132	121	122	121	133	142	146	139	139	133	115	114	111	93	83	88	81	85	84	77	87	91	90
125	121	119	123	1133	125	133	133	125	115	125	105	107	107	95	86	87	89	87	81	88	96	99	105	103
183	173	172	191	181	163	171	161	159	159	179	155	133	139	129	125	105	123	121	137	135	142	154	161	169

Figure 4-7. Computer Printout of Densities

intersect the densities in the printout. Note that the normalized densities are more or less constant in regions where the picture is smeared out. As predicted in the theory, we note that for rays horizontal or vertical, the normalized density distribution is a constant. For the other two angles, as expected, there is a variation in the normalized density distribution as shown in Figure 4-8. The distance between the maxima is approximately equal to a wavelength. The results are given in Table 4-1. The wavelength is found to be 918 Å for three of the four cases.

Reconstruction from One View, The Method of Coordinates

The use of a single picture for reconstruction involves some assumptions about the nature of the object in the picture. A reconstruction is presented in this section that involves the assumption that the density variation in the object is dependent only on the radial coordinate.[b] Thus considering the original object as a general right cylinder, each perpendicular slice is a disc having a radial density variation that is only a function of the distance to the center of the disc.

A cross-sectional slice that was divided into five concentric rings is shown in Figure 4-9. The density along each ring is assumed to be a constant. Note that the reconstruction for the right half plane can be done separately from the left half plane. However, the reconstructions will be symmetric about the z axis of the slice. The reconstruction proceeds from the basic integral equation relating the density distribution on the ith transverse slice, $\rho(\xi, \eta_i)$ to the projection $P(\eta_i)$. This is

$$\int_{S_0(\eta_i)}^{S_f(\eta_i)} \rho(\xi, \eta_i) \, d\xi = P_i(\eta_i) \qquad (4.16)$$

Symmetry allows the reconstruction of a quadrant for either the left or right half slice region of Figure 4-9. The integral of 4.16 is replaced by the finite sum involving the density rings $\rho(r_n)$ and the lengths between rings along a projection line $l_{i,n}$. Thus

$$\int_{S_0(\eta_i)}^{S_f(\eta_i)} \rho(\xi, \eta_i) \, d\xi \simeq 2 \sum_{n=1}^{N} l_{i,n} \rho_n \qquad (4.17)$$

where $\quad \rho_n = \rho(r_n), \quad n = 1, 2, 3, \ldots, N$

$\qquad N = $ number of concentric rings

[b]The calculations in the method of coordinates and the graphic outputs are due to John Harrington.

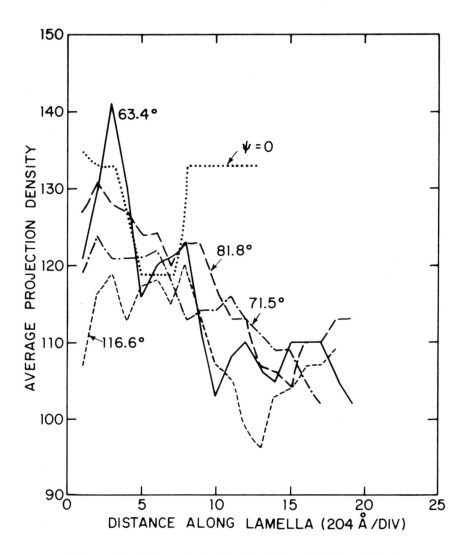

Figure 4-8. Plot of Projection Densities at Different Angles

The integral equation 4.16 has been placed in the form of N simultaneous algebraic equations in terms of the unknown densities ρ_n, $n = 1, \ldots, N$, or

$$2 \sum_{n=i}^{N} l_{i,n}\rho_n = P_i(\eta_i) = P_i \tag{4.18}$$

The matrix representation for 4.18 is

$$[L]\{\rho\} = \{P\} \tag{4.19}$$

Table 4-1
Average Distance between Maxima as a Function of Projection Angle

Angle ψ	Average Distance between Maxima
63.4°	918 Å
116.6°	918 Å
71.5°	918 Å
81.8°	——

where

$$[L] = 2 \begin{bmatrix} l_{11} & l_{12} & \cdots & l_{1,N-1} & l_{1,N} \\ 0 & l_{22} & \cdots & & l_{2,N} \\ 0 & 0 & \ddots & \vdots & l_{3,N} \\ & & & & \\ \vdots & \vdots & \ddots & l_{N-1,N-1} & \vdots \\ 0 & 0 & \cdots & 0 & l_{N,N} \end{bmatrix} \qquad (4.20)$$

$$\{\rho\} = \begin{Bmatrix} \rho_1 \\ \rho_2 \\ \vdots \\ \vdots \\ \rho_N \end{Bmatrix} \quad \text{and} \quad \{P\} = \begin{Bmatrix} P_1 \\ P_2 \\ \vdots \\ \vdots \\ P_N \end{Bmatrix} \qquad (4.21)$$

The solution of 4.19 is obtained by multiplying both sides by the inverse of 4.20 with the result

$$\{\rho\} = [L]^{-1} \{P\} \qquad (4.22)$$

As an example of the use of the method of coordinates, consider the simple linear slice density $\rho(r)$ where

$$\rho(r) = \rho_0 - (\rho_0/a)r = \rho_0 - (\rho_0/a)(\xi^2 + \eta^2)^{1/2} \qquad (4.23)$$

The radial density distribution corresponding to 4.23 is plotted along the vertical axis of Figure 4-10. The actual projection corresponding to the linear density distribution of 4.23 is shown in Figure 4-11, which is drawn for $a = 2.0$ and $\rho_0 = 4.0$. The actual projection $P(\eta)$ can be found analytically by integrating the slice density, or

$$P(\eta) = \int_{-\sqrt{a^2+\eta^2}}^{\sqrt{a^2+\eta^2}} \left[\rho_0 - \frac{\rho_0}{a} \sqrt{\xi^2 + \eta^2} \right] d\xi \qquad (4.24)$$

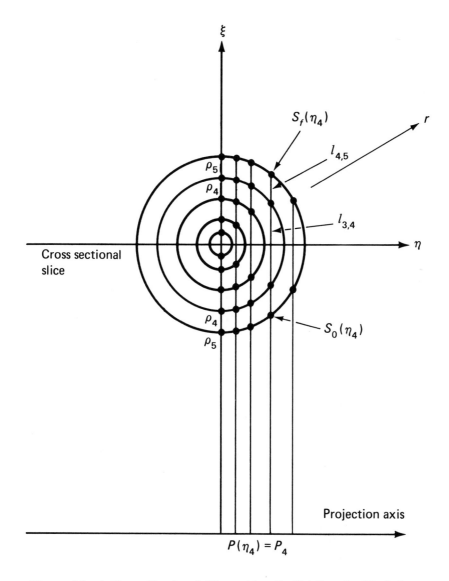

Figure 4-9. A Cross-Sectional Slice with a Radial Density Variation

$$P(\eta) = \rho_0 \sqrt{a^2 - \eta^2} \ - \ \frac{\rho_0 \eta^2}{2a} \ln\left(\frac{a + \sqrt{a^2 - \eta^2}}{a - \sqrt{a^2 - \eta^2}} \right) \qquad (4.25)$$

The projection $P(\eta)$ of 4.25 is shown in Figure 4-11.

The reconstructions for $N = 5$ and $N = 10$ are shown in Figures 4-12 and 4-13. Figure 4-12 shows the solution in a series of straight line segments and

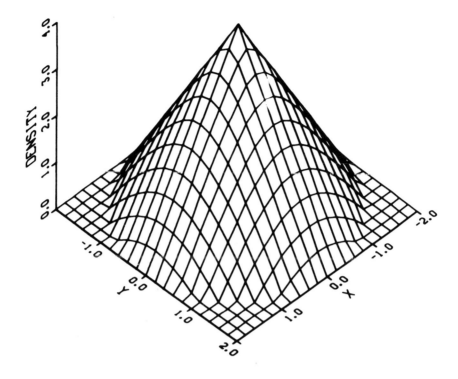

Figure 4-10. Linear Radial Density Distribution

Figure 4-13 shows the solution when the data points are connected with straight lines.

It should be noted that an angular reconstruction is possible similar to the radial distribution. In the angular case the density segments are shaped like pieces of pie. The restriction of having upper and lower half-plane symmetry is still required.

Direct Three-Dimensional Analysis of Electron Micrograph Pictures[c]

Much progress in three-dimensional reconstruction problems has been made through the use of transform techniques [2, 3]. The transform techniques work in the following way. The original electron micrographs are

[c]This section (pp. 122-134), including the illustrations, is adapted from Sandler, S., "Direct Three-dimensional Analysis of Electron Micrograph Pictures." *Pattern Recognition*, vol. 4 (1972), pp. 353-359. Used by permission of Pergamon Press Ltd.

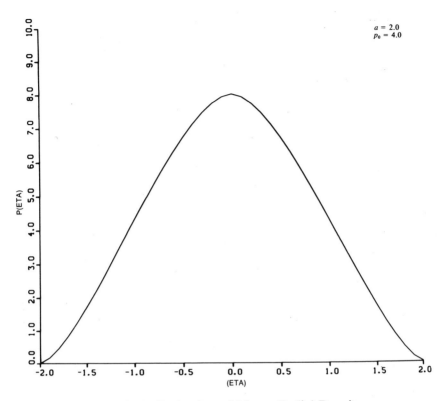

Figure 4-11. Projection of Linear Radial Density

computerized and then Fourier transformed spatially. The complete transform space must be filled in either by taking a full hemisphere of pictures or by using the known symmetry properties of the specimen. Objects that have a long axis are reconstructed by obtaining a series of rotation pictures. Since the angular range of the electron micrograph rotation goniometer is limited, only a restricted angular range is possible. The known symmetry properties are introduced and a series of two-dimensional Fourier transforms are calculated for each transverse segment. These transforms are then retransformed and stacked in the longitudinal direction for the complete three-dimensional reconstruction.

Two parts of the process need to be emphasized here. (1) The inverse Fourier transformation cannot be performed unless the relevant space is completely filled in. Thus, a limited number of views of an object with no known crystallographic symmetry is not possible. (2) The reconstructions are unique in that the transforms are unique, i.e., one and only one object is possible for a complete set of projections and their projection transforms.

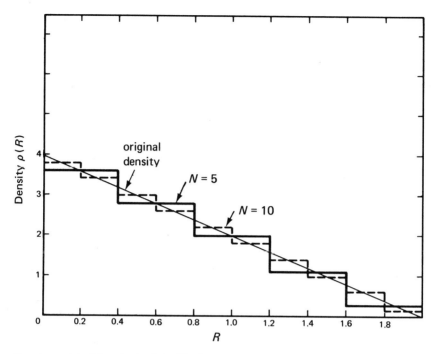

Based on original drawing by John Harrington.

Figure 4-12. Reconstruction with Discontinuous Straight Line Segments

This section is addressed to the problem of directly and uniquely determining a structure from a set of different views of the object [8]. The present work is confined to structures that may be reconstructed by stacking transverse sections along the axis of rotation.

The Formulation of the Problem

The general problem is pictorially represented in Figure 4-14. The relation between the two-dimensional density distribution on the ith transverse segment $\rho(\xi, \eta_i)$ and its projection on the electron micrograph plate is

$$\int_{S_0(\eta_i)}^{S_f(\eta_i)} \rho(\xi, \eta_i) \, d\xi = P_i(\eta_i) \tag{4.26}$$

The subscript i indicates that the projection corresponds to rotation angle ψ_i where $0 \le \psi_i \le \pi$, $i = 1, 2, 3, \ldots, N$. The result is to have a set of N cou-

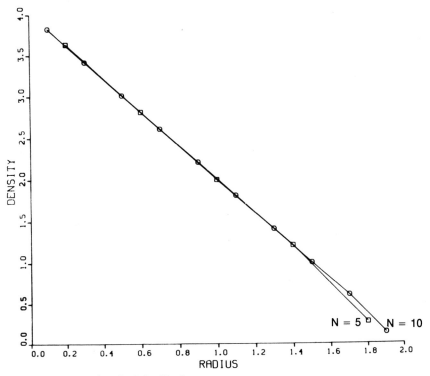

UNIFORM DENSITY BANDS

Based on computations by John Harrington.

Figure 4-13. Reconstruction When Data Points Are Connected with Straight Lines

pled integral equations between the projections and the density distribution ρ. Thus, the reconstruction problem reduces to the following:

$$\left. \begin{array}{c} \displaystyle\int_{S_0(\eta_1)}^{S_f(\eta_1)} \rho(\xi, \eta_1) \, d\xi = P_1(\eta_1) \\[3em] \displaystyle\int_{S_0(\eta_2)}^{S_f(\eta_2)} \rho(\xi, \eta_2) \, d\xi = P_2(\eta_2) \\[3em] \vdots \\[3em] \displaystyle\int_{S_0(\eta_N)}^{S_f(\eta_N)} \rho(\xi, \eta_N) \, d\xi = P_N(\eta_N) \end{array} \right\} \qquad (4.27)$$

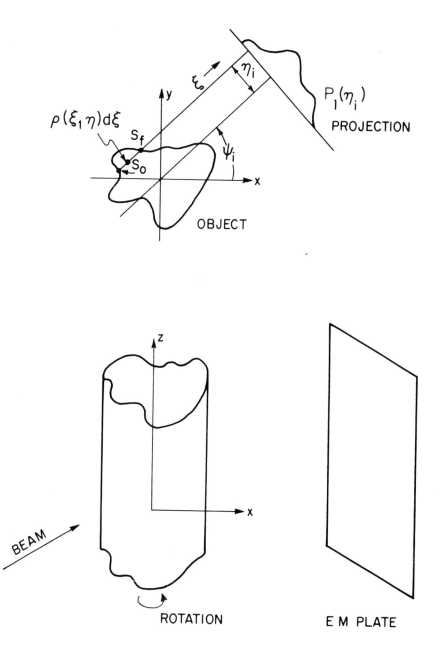

Figure 4-14. The Geometry Used for Reconstruction of Transmission Images on an Electron Microscope That Has a Rotation Stage

The case where the object is a disc with complete symmetry can be solved by means of Abel's integral equation. Since all projections of a disc with only radial dependence are identical, only one equation of the set 4.27 is needed.

Although a general formula has been presented for the integral equations [1], no results were presented, nor does it seem possible to apply the general result of the authors. Gordon, Bender, and Herman [7] have presented a method that appears to give a good representation of the object. Their basic method will be presented later. The method presented here differs in that it gives a unique solution. Vainshtein et al [10] have also given some ideas on real space reconstruction, but the method does not seem to be generally applicable.

The Solution of the Problem

The requirement for a solution is that a unique relation must be given between the projections and the two-dimensional density distributions. The prescription must also specify the number and location of the required views and the number of data points needed from each view. A few simple examples will show that it is by no means a trivial problem to construct a geometry in which a unique solution is possible. Consider the system of Figure 4-15 in which four densities, ρ_i, $i = 1, 2, 3, 4$ are located at the corners of a square. If the projections are taken at right angles, then it is possible to present more than one density distribution that satisfies the projection values. This is due to the fact that the four equations that relate the projections to their densities are not independent. Actually, the equation for ρ_4 can be obtained from the remaining three equations. When the projections are separated by 45° as shown in Figure 4-16, the situation is changed. A unique relation may now be presented which relates the projections and the densities. These are given below in algebraic and matrix form.

$$
\begin{aligned}
\rho_1 \quad &+ \rho_3 \quad &&= P_1 \\
\rho_2 \quad &\quad + \rho_4 &&= P_2 \\
\rho_1 \quad &\quad &&= P_3 \\
\rho_2 + \rho_3 \quad &\quad &&= P_4
\end{aligned}
\tag{4.28}
$$

The system 4.28 is given in matrix form as

$$[\Phi]\{\rho\} = \{P\} \tag{4.29}$$

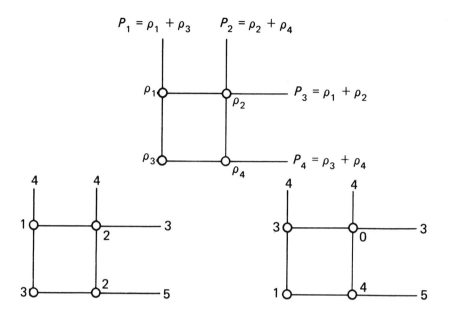

Figure 4-15. Reconstruction of Four Density Points with Two Views Separated by 90 Degrees

where

$$[\Phi] = \begin{bmatrix} 1 & 0 & 1 & 0 \\ 0 & 1 & 0 & 1 \\ 1 & 0 & 0 & 0 \\ 0 & 1 & 1 & 0 \end{bmatrix} \quad \{\rho\} = \begin{Bmatrix} \rho_1 \\ \rho_2 \\ \rho_3 \\ \rho_4 \end{Bmatrix} \text{ and } \{P\} = \begin{Bmatrix} P_1 \\ P_2 \\ P_3 \\ P_4 \end{Bmatrix} \tag{4.30}$$

The explicit solution for the four densities ρ_1, $i = 1, 2, 3, 4$, is

$$\{\rho\} = [\Phi]^{-1} \{P\} \tag{4.31}$$

where

$$[\Phi]^{-1} = \begin{bmatrix} 0 & 0 & 1 & 0 \\ -1 & 0 & 1 & 1 \\ 1 & 0 & -1 & 0 \\ 1 & 1 & -1 & -1 \end{bmatrix} \tag{4.32}$$

The reason the system of Figure 4-16 gives a unique result is that the

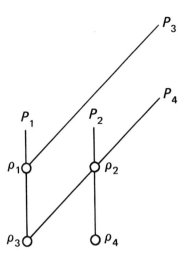

Figure 4-16. Reconstruction of Four Density Points with Two Views Separated by 45 Degrees

determinant of Φ is not zero, whereas that corresponding to Figure 4-15 is identically zero. A zero determinant indicates that the matrix of coefficients Φ is defective and that the N equations are mutually dependent. Consider the system of Figure 4-17. Here the projection lines are drawn in the following way. For each projection P_i a line is drawn which goes through ρ_i. The geometry is chosen so that all line intersections lie either on the density locations or on neutral points between them. There are three views required for the 3×3 arrangement of Figure 4-17, with mutual separations of $45°$. The total angular range of needed views is $90°$. If views are taken within this range but not on the precise location angles, they may be easily interpolated onto the "normal" coordinates. Note that the geometry is only topological in that a 3×3 arrangement of points in a rectangular array would require less than or greater than $90°$ of views depending on whether rotation is about the long or short axis. A more convenient geometry for the 3×3 array is shown in Figure 4-18, where each point is replaced by a square. The same type of unique relation is found for both cases. An example for the geometry of Figure 4-18 is worked out in the following section. Note that the original densities are computed exactly by this method.

Numerical Example

Consider the geometry shown in Figure 4-18a where the area densities have the following values:

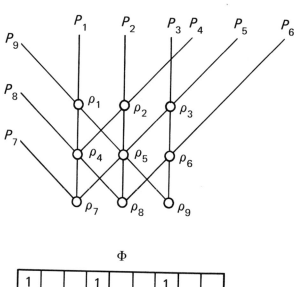

Figure 4-17. The Geometry and Transformation Matrices That Relate 9 Density Points and 9 Projections

$$\begin{Bmatrix} \rho_1 \\ \rho_2 \\ \rho_3 \\ \rho_4 \\ \rho_5 \\ \rho_6 \\ \rho_7 \\ \rho_8 \\ \rho_9 \end{Bmatrix} = \begin{Bmatrix} 1 \\ 2 \\ 3 \\ 4 \\ 5 \\ 6 \\ 7 \\ 8 \\ 9 \end{Bmatrix} \qquad (4.33)$$

$$\Phi^{-1}$$

3/2	1	1/2	−1	−1/2	−1/2	−1	−1/2	−1/2
1/2	1	1/2	0	−1/2	−1/2	0	−1/2	−1/2
1	1	1	−1	0	−1	−1	0	−1
−1/2	−1	−1/2	1	1/2	1/2	0	1/2	1/2
−1	−1	−1	1	1	1	0	0	1
−1/2	−1	−1/2	1	1/2	1/2	0	−1/2	1/2
0	0	0	0	0	0	1	0	0
1/2	1	1/2	−1	−1/2	−1/2	0	1/2	−1/2
−1/2	0	1/2	0	−1/2	−1/2	1	1/2	1/2

Figure 4-17. (Continued)

The corresponding projection values are

$$\begin{Bmatrix} P_1 \\ P_2 \\ P_3 \\ P_4 \\ P_5 \\ P_6 \\ P_7 \\ P_8 \\ P_9 \end{Bmatrix} = \begin{Bmatrix} 12 \\ 15 \\ 18 \\ 6\sqrt{2} \\ 15\sqrt{2} \\ 14\sqrt{2} \\ 7\sqrt{2} \\ 12\sqrt{2} \\ 15\sqrt{2} \end{Bmatrix} \qquad (4.34)$$

The original density values are found by multiplying the matrix of Figure 4-18b by the column projection matrix in 4.34. Thus,

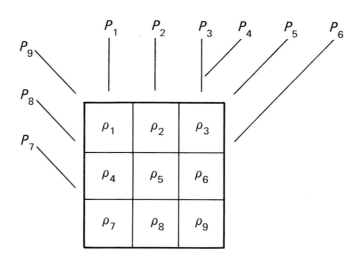

$$S = \sqrt{2}$$

Figure 4-18a. Geometry and Corresponding Matrix for 9 Area Densities and 9 Projections

$$\Phi^{-1}$$

1.5000	1.0000	0.5000	-0.7071	-0.3535	-0.3535	-0.7071	-0.3535	-0.3535
0.5000	1.0000	0.5000	0	-0.3535	-0.3535	0	-0.3535	-0.3535
1.0000	1.0000	1.0000	-0.7071	0	-0.7071	-0.7071	0	-0.7071
-0.5000	-1.0000	-0.5000	0.7071	0.3535	0.3535	0	0.3535	0.3535
-1.0000	-1.0000	-1.0000	0.7071	0.7071	0.7071	0	0	0.7071
-0.5000	-1.0000	-0.5000	0.7071	0.3535	1.0606	0	-0.3535	0.3535
0	0	0	0	0	0	0.7071	0	0
0.5000	1.0000	0.5000	-0.7071	-0.3535	-0.3535	0	0.3535	-0.3535
-0.5000	0	0.5000	0	-0.3535	-0.3535	0.7071	0.3535	0.3535

Figure 4-18b. Transformation Matrix That Relates 9 Area Densities and 9 Projections

$$[\Phi]^{-1}\{P\} = \{\rho\} = \begin{Bmatrix} 1 \\ 2 \\ 3 \\ 4 \\ 5 \\ 6 \\ 7 \\ 8 \\ 9 \end{Bmatrix} \tag{4.35}$$

Note that the result 4.35 is identical with the original densities in 4.33.

Algebraic Reconstruction Techniques

One very important method of reconstruction was given by Gordon, Bender, and Herman in 1970 [7]. This method was given the name ART, meaning Algebraic Reconstruction Technique, and works directly with the projection pictures. The technique begins with an original guess for the structure densities and uses a mathematical algorithm to improve the guess. The initial guess here is the mean density of the object. The algorithm is then used iteratively on the initial estimate, so as to satisfy the projection pictures at each step. The projection equations used by Gordon, et al., were written in terms of a ray, $R_{k\theta}$, and a two-dimensional density ρ_{ij}, where

$$\rho_{ij} = \rho(i, j) \quad \begin{aligned} i &= 1, 2, 3, \ldots, n \\ j &= 1, 2, 3, \ldots, n \end{aligned} \tag{4.36}$$

The ray $R_{k\theta}$ is a band of width w, located at an angle θ. Since the ray is finite in width, the projection of the ray, $P_{k\theta}^r$, may or may not be equal to the actual projection, $P_{k\theta}^a$. The ray $P_{k\theta}^r$ is called the pseudoprojection for this reason [5]. The projection equation for each ray $R_{k\theta}$ is

$$P_{k\theta}^r = \sum \rho_{ij} \tag{4.37}$$

where the sum is taken over all points in the ray. The multiplicative method uses the following algorithm to produce an improved approximation for the density ρ_{ij}^{p+1} beginning from a previous density ρ_{ij}^{p}

$$\rho_{ij}^{p+1} = \left[\frac{P_{k\theta}^a}{P_{k\theta}^r} \right] \rho_{ij}^{p} \tag{4.38}$$

One advantage of the multiplicative algorithm 4.38 is that it always produces an improved density that is greater than zero. The additive algorithm given by Gordon, et al., can give rise to negative densities, which must be set equal to zero. The algorithm 4.38 automatically adjusts the object densities to satisfy one projection exactly. The error in the reconstruction can then be determined by comparing the reconstructed result with the projection or picture that is not satisfied exactly. The iterative process is terminated when the error in reconstruction is less than a predetermined value. Gordon, et al., use the concept of Euclidean "distance" in computing the error in the density reconstructions [7]. This distance is the mean square error in the density reconstruction, averaged over the number of points. The type of error analysis is valid only when one has access to the actual densities within the object. Another approach is more useful when one only has access to projection data. Here the mean square error between the actual projection and the reconstructed projection is relevant.

It is not necessary to use rays in doing a reconstruction. In fact, the use of the ray can be a source of error. These errors are due to the facts that the ray width varies as a function of the projection angle and that the ray method is unstable unless all pictures are consistent [5]. These errors can be avoided by using discrete density points.

Consider now the detailed theory for a two-picture reconstruction, where the cross-sectional densities are laid out on a grid. The grid is formed by the densitometered projection values, formed by two line scans.

The following two projection equations form the basis of the reconstruction problem

$$\int_{S_0(\eta_1)}^{S_f(\eta_1)} \rho(\xi, \eta_1) \, d\xi = P_1(\eta_1) \tag{4.39}$$

$$\int_{S_0(\eta_2)}^{S_f(\eta_2)} \rho(\xi, \eta_2) \, d\xi = P_2(\eta_2) \tag{4.40}$$

Consider the two lined up pictures to be represented by $P_1(l, k)$ and $P_2(l, j)$ where

l = line number on the photograph

$$j = 1, 2, 3, \ldots, r_j \tag{4.41}$$

$k = 1, 2, 3, \ldots, l_k; \quad l_k = r_j \cos \psi$

The geometry for reconstructing a single slice is shown in Figure 4-19. A suitable zeroth-order approximation for the object density ρ is

$$\rho(l, j, k) = \alpha(k) P_1(l, k) P_2(l, j) \tag{4.42}$$

The constant $\alpha(k)$ is found by solving the projection equation 4.40. It is given by

$$\alpha(k) = \left[\Delta_1 \sum_{j=n_k}^{m_k} P_2(l, j) \right]^{-1}, \quad k = 1, 2, 3, \ldots, l_k \tag{4.43}$$

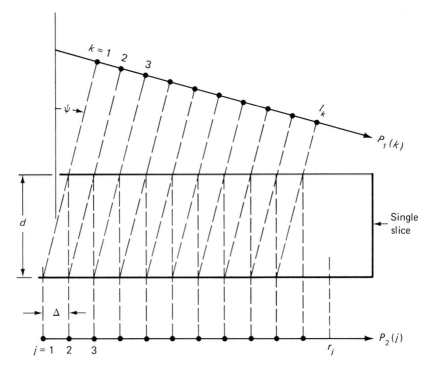

Δ = Raster size
d = Specimen thickness
ψ = Rotation angle

Figure 4-19. Geometry for Reconstructing a Single Slice

where $n_1 = 1$, $n_k = n_{k-1} + \Delta/\cos\psi$; $m_1 = (d/\Delta)\sin\psi$, $m_k = m_{k-1} + \Delta/\cos\psi$; and $\Delta_1 = \Delta/\sin\psi$ = incremental length in j direction.

The densities ρ now satisfy projection one. They must be made to satisfy projection two. The densities are then integrated along the projection lines for $P_2(j)$, and a constant correction factor is found. The new corrected densities are

$$\rho_{\text{new}}(l, j, k) = \rho_{\text{old}}(l, j, k)P_2(l, j)\,[P_2'(l, j)]^{-1} \qquad (4.44)$$

where $\quad P_2'(l, j) = \Delta_2 \sum_{k_L}^{k_U} \rho_{\text{old}}(l, j, k)$

and $\quad \Delta_2 = \Delta/\tan\psi$

$\qquad k_U = 1 + (j - 1)\cos\psi$

$\qquad k_L = k_U - (d/\Delta)\sin\psi$

The new densities must now satisfy the P_1 projection. The constant correction factor for each projection line is found by integrating along the P_1 projection lines. The new slice densities ρ are given by setting $\rho_{new}(l, j, k)$ above equal to $\rho_{old}(l, j, k)$. They are

$$\rho_{new}(l, j, k) = \rho_{old}(l, j, k)P_1(l, k)[P_1'(l, k)]^{-1} \qquad (4.45)$$

where $\quad P_1'(l, k) = \Delta_1 \sum_{j_L}^{j_U} \rho_{old}(l, j, k)$

and $\quad j_L = 1 + (k - 1)/\cos\psi$

$\qquad j_U = j_L + (d/\Delta)\tan\psi$

The process is repeated until the correction term has reached a predetermined small value. The entire object is reconstructed by repeating the entire process for all lines with index l.

Iterative Techniques

The purpose of this section is to show the application of a direct reconstruction method to a particular biological object. The object is a posterior central segment of the human corneal stroma. The result is the three-dimensional reconstruction of the fibrils within a particular lamella. The cornea consists of roughly parallel fibrils that are contained in lamellas. The adjacent lamellas are displaced in angle from one another as one moves from the posterior to the anterior region [4]. The basic theory is presented here along with the special methods employed to line up and computer process the information.

The Theory Used for Reconstruction[d]

The basic problem here is to reconstruct a three-dimensional structure from a limited number of views. The views are transmission pictures taken with an electron microscope. Theoretically, a complete 180° hemisphere of views is needed to perform a unique three-dimensional reconstruction. The practical problems involved in the construction of electron microscopes limit the useful range of available angles. Tilt angles of 30° are common. Two possible choices are (1) to make sufficient assumptions about the nature of the object to allow reconstruction, or (2) to work with the available data in the most efficient way. The latter approach is chosen here. The

[d]This section (pp. 137-151), including all illustrations except Figure 4-28, is a revised, expanded version of Sandler, S., "Direct Three-dimensional Reconstruction of a Corneal Stromal Lamella." *Journal of Theoretical Biology*, vol. 48 (1974), pp. 207-213. Used by permission of Academic Press Inc. (London) Limited.

reconstruction is devised such that the three-dimensional object (i.e., a lamella of the corneal stroma) is found that can produce the pictures appearing on the electron micrograph plates.

Many researchers have been involved with theoretical treatments relative to direct reconstruction methods. Theories have been proposed by Berry and Gibbs [1], Gordon et al., [7], Sandler [8], and Gilbert [6]. The reader is encouraged to consult these works.

The basic geometry used for reconstruction is shown in Figure 4-20. The object (shown in Figure 4-21) is aligned along a suitable long axis. A goniometer stage in the electron microscope accomplishes this purpose. The object can be considered as a stack of flat slices, each perpendicular to the axis of rotation. The transmission picture corresponding to each slice is a line. The optical density along the line is used with a corresponding gray scale to be visualized as a picture. The complete set of lines forms the electron micrograph or transmission picture corresponding to the object. A rotation of the object by some angle about the axis produces another picture. Two such rotation pictures can be used for three-dimensional reconstruction by finding the two-dimensional slice from the corresponding picture lines and then stacking the slices. The reconstruction method for more than two pictures proceeds in the same way as for two pictures. The multi-picture reconstruction is accomplished by considering the pictures two at a time.

The reconstruction method is quite simple to understand in a general way. The details in the method are given later in this section. The relation between the two-dimensional density distribution on a transverse segment and its projection on the electron micrograph plate is

$$\int_{S_0(\eta_i)}^{S_f(\eta_i)} \rho(\xi, \eta_i) \, d\xi = P_i(\eta_i) \tag{4.46}$$

The subscript i corresponds to the rotation angle ψ_0. The two-view problem consists of solving the following two simultaneous integral equations:

$$\int_{S_0(\eta_1)}^{S_f(\eta_1)} \rho(\xi, \eta_1) \, d\xi = P_1(\eta_1) \tag{4.47}$$

and

$$\int_{S_0(\eta_2)}^{S_f(\eta_2)} \rho(\xi, \eta_2) \, d\xi = P_2(\eta_2) \tag{4.48}$$

where $S_0(\eta)$ and $S_f(\eta)$ are the extrema of the projection line. The basic procedure for the reconstruction is to begin with an approximate solution to 4.47 and 4.48 and to improve the result by a properly chosen iteration

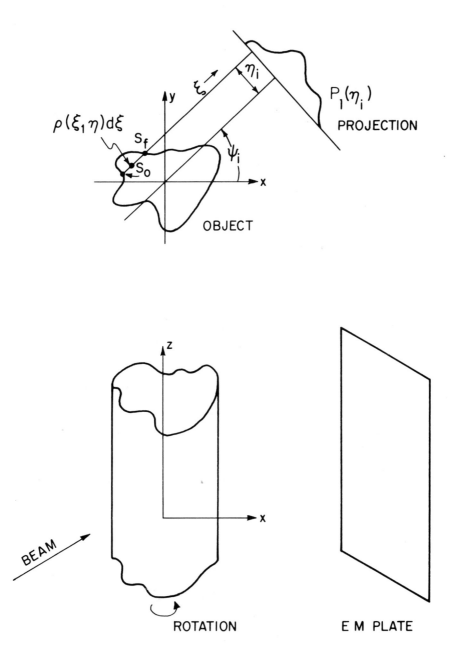

Figure 4-20. Basic Geometry for Reconstructing an Object on an Electron Microscope. The rotation angle refers to the gonimeter axis.

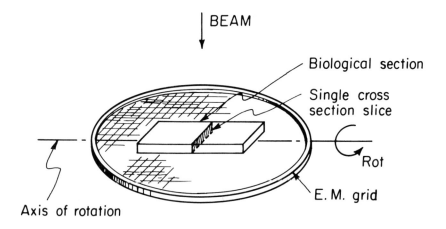

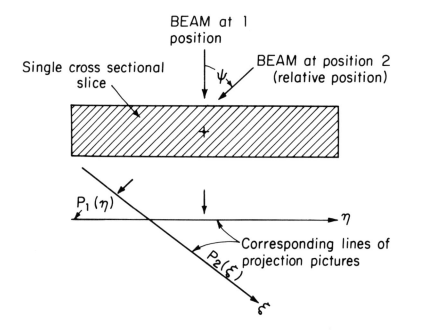

Figure 4-21. The Physical Position of the Biological Section on the Grid. Its cross section is shown in the lower figure.

method. The zeroth-order solution to 4.47 that satisfies the integral equation is

$$\rho_1^{(0)} (\xi, \eta_1) = \alpha P_1 (\eta_1) P_2 (\xi) \qquad (4.49)$$

The zeroth-order solution 4.49 was chosen to give a reasonable representation for the actual density variation. The success of this direct method depends on a proper guess for the density distribution. The improved solutions are obtained by an iterative solution of 4.47 and 4.48. The value of α in 4.49 is chosen so as to satisfy the relevant density equation 4.47. It then has the value

$$\alpha = \left[\int P_2(\xi)\, d\xi \right]^{-1} \tag{4.50}$$

The other projection equation 4.48 is satisfied by adding up the densities of 4.47 and 4.48 in the direction of the second projection. The original densities are modified by a single multiplicative constant to satisfy 4.48 exactly. These densities are then used to compute the new values for the first projection. Any difference is accounted for by a new single multiplicative constant. The process is then repeated until the desired error is obtained. Figure 4-22 shows the process diagrammatically.

An example of the method is shown in Figure 4-23. The segment chosen corresponds to a transverse cornea segment which projects on the electron micrograph plate as a longitudinal view of the lamella. Two projection lines are shown displaced 30° from one another. The optical densities corresponding to the projections are plotted at right angles. The computer-generated reconstruction for two and four iterations is plotted in Figure 4-24 and compares favorably with the actual two-dimensional density distribution. Note that the reconstruction is best when the relatively dense objects are clearly separated. This is not a severe limitation since the cross section of the fibrils is known, and the relative orientation of the fibrils changes in the direction of the fibril axis.

The Reconstruction of the Posterior Section of the Corneal Stroma

The basic material for study was taken from osmium-fixed, epon-embedded samples of central human cornea.[e] A block was prepared by cutting out a small piece from the posterior region of the central cornea. This small piece was remounted after noting the orientation of the lamellas on a section prepared for light microscopy. The microtome knife could then be properly positioned to cut sections in which the collagens run in transverse and longitudinal directions in adjacent lamellas. The sections were examined on an electron microscope fitted with a ±30° goniometer. Suitable sections were found in which the collagens in the adjacent lamellas were orthogonal to each other. The axis of the goniometer was then lined up with the collagens of the longitudinal lamella. A dirt spot was used as a

---

[e] These blocks were prepared and supplied by Dr. Ben S. Fine, Ophthalmic Pathology Branch, Armed Forces Institute of Pathology, Washington, D.C.

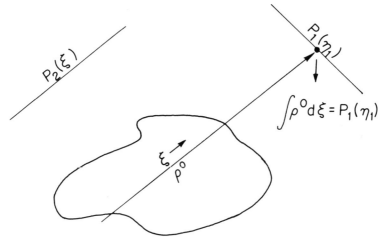

STEP 1. ρ^O found by sweeping out $P_1(\eta_1)$
according to $P_2(\xi)$

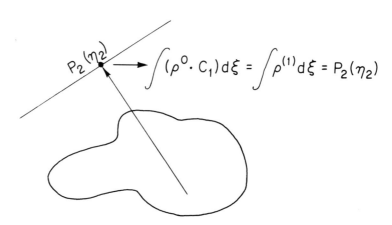

STEP 2. Zeroth order solution modified by
constant C_1 to satisfy the second projection.
(Use projection lines for P_2).

Figure 4-22. The Direct Reconstruction Process Shown Diagramatically

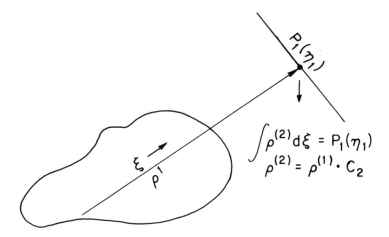

$$\int \rho^{(2)} d\xi = P_1(\eta_1)$$
$$\rho^{(2)} = \rho^{(1)} \cdot C_2$$

<u>STEP 3.</u> The first order solution is modified by a new constant C_2 to satisfy the first projection. (Use projection lines for P_1)

<u>Remaining Steps.</u> Steps (2) and (3) are repeated using the last found approximation for the densities.

Figure 4-22. (Continued)

reference to rotate the section through 30°. The two resulting pictures are shown in Figures 4-25 and 4-26.

Figures 4-25 and 4-26 indicate the collagen fibrils appear to be weaving in and out. This conclusion is drawn by looking at the fibrils in the *transverse* section. The 0° picture shows the collagen fibrils as dots indicating that they are seen head on. Actually they have the three-dimensional appearance of short cylinders with lengths equal to the section thickness on the grid (i.e., about two fibril diameters thick). The 30° picture shows that the relative orientation of the fibril segments is not related in any simple way to the longitudinal section. A single angular relation between the fibrils of two adjacent lamellas would predict a uniform orientation for the fibrils of the transverse segment. It is not possible to make any conclusions about the nature of the fibrillar weaving from Figures 4-25 and 4-26 because of the finite thickness of the grid sections which allow one longitudinal fibril to be superimposed on another.

The longitudinal sections of the two photographs are lined up in Figure

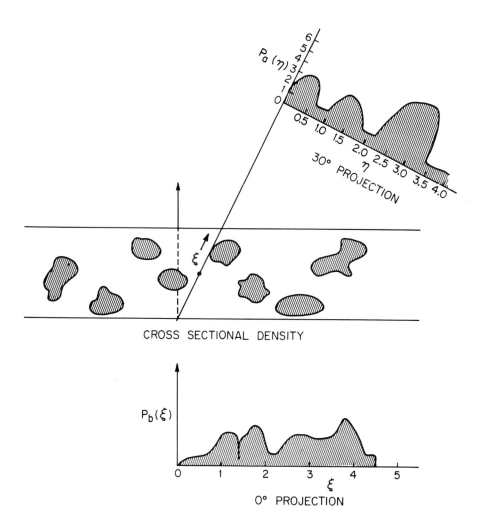

Figure 4-23. The Projections That Correspond to 0° and 30° Views of a Cross-sectional Slice

4-27 for reconstruction. The photographs were lined up by imaging them with a stereoscope. The photographs were considered lined up when the best three-dimensional perception of the individual fibrils was obtained. The long axis alignment is relatively simple since the dirt spot is used as a reference. The alignment along the transverse direction was checked in the computer by trying small and large shifts in the angular orientation of the two pictures. The results showed that the reconstruction only converged

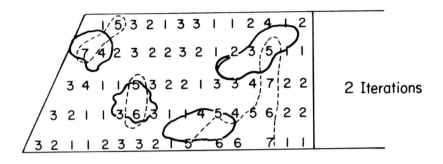

2 Iterations

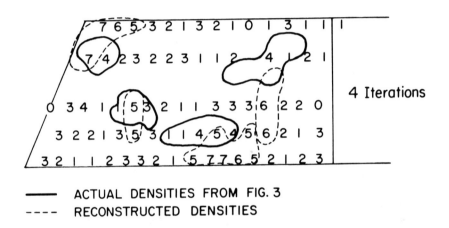

4 Iterations

——— ACTUAL DENSITIES FROM FIG. 3
- - - - RECONSTRUCTED DENSITIES

Figure 4-24. The Computer-generated Densities for the Cross-sectional Slice

for a very narrow region about the predicted transverse (i.e., angular) picture orientation. Convergence was not possible for other values of transverse shifts between the pictures. The theory of the preceding section can be used directly on the composite. Densitometry of the composite photograph gave the basic line-to-line information needed for reconstruction. The projection lines needed for reconstruction were the corresponding P_1 and P_2 lines in equations 4.47 and 4.48.

A sample computer output from an IBM 360-75 for a single rectangular disc slice is shown in Figure 4-28. The pages of output were combined by stacking to make a three-dimensional model. A drawing of the model is

146

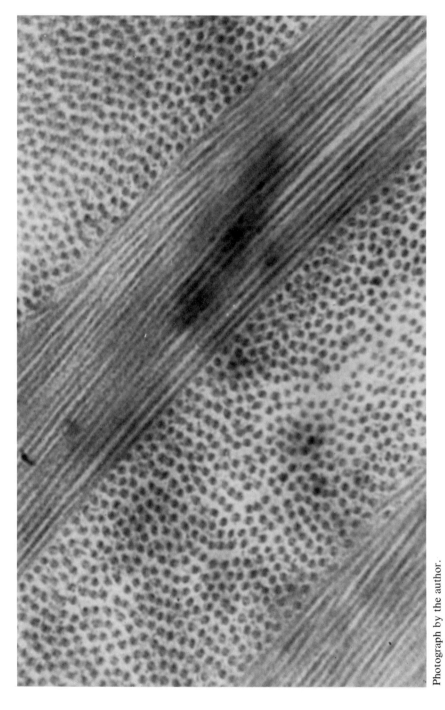

Photograph by the author.

Figure 4-25. A 0° Transmission Picture of a Sample of Posterior Human Corneal Stroma

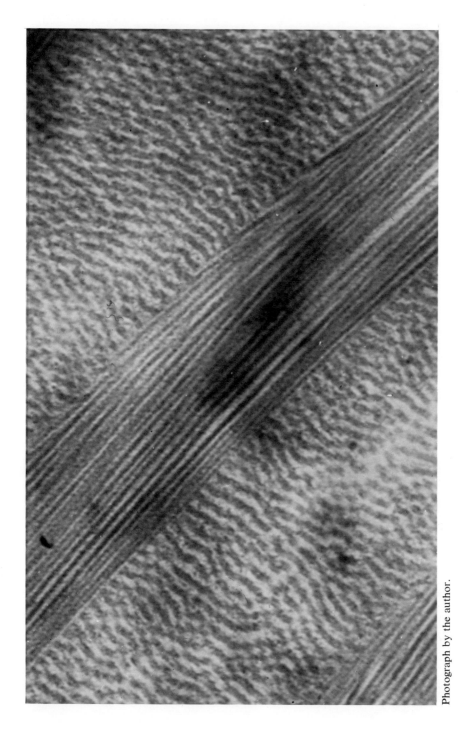

Photograph by the author.

Figure 4-26. A 30° Transmission Picture of a Sample of Posterior Human Corneal Stroma

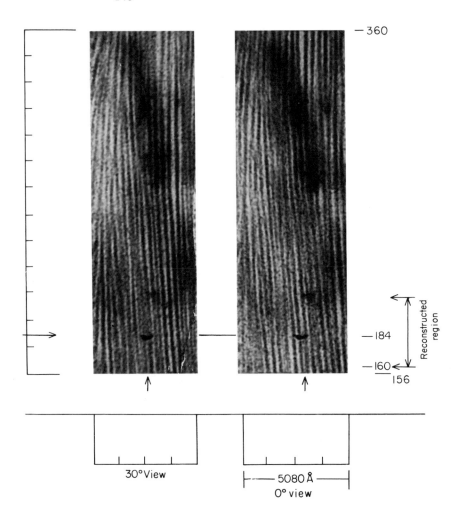

Figure 4-27. A Lined-up Composite Picture of Corresponding Sections of a Lamella

shown in Figure 4-29. This model was drawn as an isometric projection by transcribing the computer outputs onto the horizontal planes of the drawing. The intersections on each horizontal plane were connected with cylinders. The result could be smoothed somewhat, but it was felt that the raw result would be more representative of the method.

Note that there is a definite variation in the longitudinal position of fibrils about the plane of section. It is not a case in which fibrils themselves are parallel and go obliquely through the section. Figure 4-29 shows that

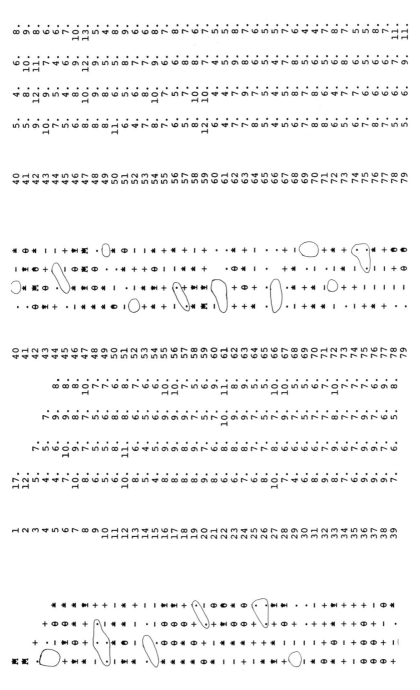

Figure 4-28. A Computer Section of the Cross-sectional Density of a Corneal Slice

150

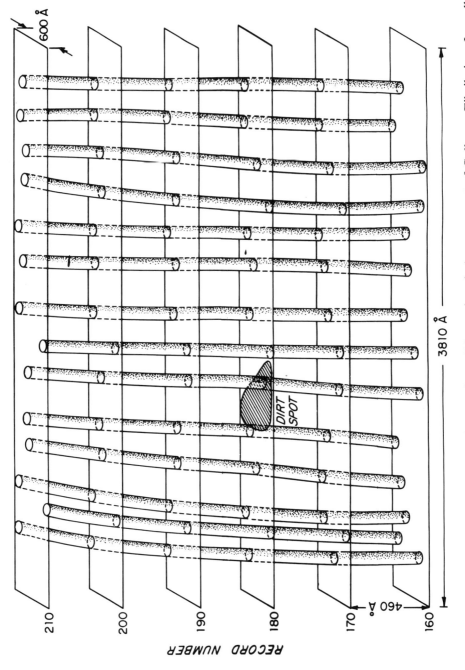

Figure 4-29. An Isometric Drawing of the Three-Dimensional Arrangement of Collagen Fibrils in a Lamella

there are fibrils that are relatively straight, others that are oblique, and still others that appear to weave in and out.

The searching procedure for examining the sections did not disclose any lamellas having parallel fibrils along their lengths. Sections were prepared from blocks by remounting the blocks and cutting slices that were oblique to the previous cuts. As examination of these oblique cuts also did not disclose any individual lamellas with parallel fibrils.

References

1. Berry, M.V., and Gibbs, R. "The Interpretation of Optical Projections." *Proceedings of the Royal Society*, London, vol. 314A, no. 1517 (1970), pp. 143-152.

2. Crowther, R.A.; DeRosier, D.J.; and Klug, A. "Reconstruction of Spherical Viruses by Fourier Synthesis from Electron Micrographs." *Nature*, vol. 226 (1970), pp. 421-425.

3. DeRosier, D.J., and Klug, A. "Reconstruction of Three-Dimensional Structures from Electron Micrographs." *Nature*, vol. 217 (1968), pp. 130-136.

4. Fine, B.S., and Yanoff, M. *Ocular Histology, A Text and Atlas*. New York: Harper & Row Publishers, 1972, pp. 150-155.

5. Gilbert, P.F.C. "Iterative Methods for the Three-dimensional Reconstruction of an Object from Projections." *Journal of Theoretical Biology*, vol. 36 (1972), pp. 107-117.

6. Gilbert, P.F.C. "The Reconstruction of a Three-dimensional Structure from Projections and Its Application to Electron Microscopy II Direct Method." *Proceedings of the Royal Society*, London, vol. B182, no. 89 (1972), pp. 89-102.

7. Gordon, R.; Bender, R.; and Herman, G.T. "Algebraic Reconstruction Techniques for Three-dimensional Electron Microscopy and X-ray Photography." *Journal of Theoretical Biology*, vol. 29 (1970), pp. 471-481.

8. Sandler, S.S. "Direct Three-dimensional Analysis of Electron Micrograph Pictures." *Pattern Recognition*, vol. 4 (1972), pp. 353-359.

9. Sandler, S.S. "Direct Three-dimensional Reconstruction of a Posterior Section of the Human Corneal Stroma from Electron Micrographs." *Journal of Theoretical Biology*, vol. 48 (1974), pp. 207-213.

10. Vainshtein, B.K.; Baryner, V.V.; and Guiskaya, C.V. "The Hexagonal Crystalline Structure of Catalase and Its Molecular Structure." *Soviet Physics Doklady*, vol. 13 (1969), pp. 838-841.

Appendix

The program given here was used to generate the cross-sectional "slices" used to reconstruct the object shown in Figure 4-29.[a] The original photographs shown in Figure 4-27 were densitometered on an Optronics machine with the output recorded on a magnetic tape. The readings are unpacked by the command READ (OUTTP,4). Each line of the picture contains information for the two views described on page 000. The name IOFST refers to the offset needed to line up the pictures. The labels used in this program are in general consistent with the theory given on page 000 et seq. For example,

$$DELK = \Delta_k$$

$$DELJ = \Delta_j$$

The convergence in the iteration procedure was determined by finding the error between the predicted and actual projections. The specified error is given by EPS, and is related to the sum of the projection values for each line. The gray scale printing is done at the end of the program by overprinting.

```
C      DIMENSION OD(2600,30),RECX(30),LOD(5200,30),IBEG(10),IEND(10),
       DIMENSION OD(2600,2 ),RECX(30),LOD(5200,2 ),IBEG(10),IEND(10),
      1RHO(100,100),ALPH(100),AIDEN(35),IOFST(10),ORC(100),ORB(100)
      2,AOUT(15),ATWO(15),ANB(40)
       COMMON OD,RECX
       INTEGER*2 OD,RECX
       INTEGER*4 OUTTP/9/ ,AINCR
       LOGICAL*1 LOD
       EQUIVALENCE (LOD(1,1),OD(1,1))
CCC
CC  DATA CARD READS IN CHARACTERS FOR OUTPUT, COL 2,3 OVERPRINT FOR
CC          INTENSITY = 0, COL 4,5 FOR INTENS = 1,..., COL 26,27 FOR 12
       READ (5,2071)  (ANB(II), II=1,26)
 2071 FORMAT ( 1X,40A1)
CCC    I1IS FIRST RECORD     I2 IS LAST    I3 IS INPUT RECORD LENGTH
CCC    I3IS INPUT RECORD LENGTH A2   IE ONE HALF LENGTH IN BYTES
CC        DUMP9
       READ(5,3) I1,I2,I3
    3 FORMAT (10I4)
       READ (5,1051) NFILM,D,DELTA,THETA,EPS,AIDEN
       READ (5,3) (IOFST(JJ),JJ=2,NFILM)
       READ(5,2222) LK
 2222 FORMAT(I4)
CCCCC
CCCCC     NFILM CAN ONLY BE 2 NOW     SEE 2000 COMMENT CCCCCC
CCCCC
 1051 FORMAT (I5,4F10.5,35A1)
       MREC=I1
       I113 = 2*I3
       WRITE (6,10) NFILM,AIDEN,I1,I2,I3,I113,D,DELTA,THETA,EPS
```

[a]This program was written by Barbara Sandler.

```
   10 FORMAT (1HO,I6,' FILMS,  DATA ID: ',35A1//'  FIRST RECORD = ',
     1I4,',   LAST RECORD =',I4/'   I3 =',I4,',  RECORD LENGTH, BYTES ='
     2,I4//'   D =',F10.5/'   DELTA =',F10.5/'    THETA =',F10.5/
     3'    EPS =',F10.5/)
      IW=I1/30
      IS=I2/30
CCC
CCC    SKIPS OUT TO RECORD DESIRED
      IF(I1-1) 28,28,25
   25 DO 1 K=1,I1
      I = 1
      READ(OUTTP,4) RECX(I),(OD(J,I),J=1,I3)
    4 FORMAT(250A2,250A2,250A2,250A2,250A2,250A2,250A2,250A2,152A2
     1)
    2 CONTINUE
    1 CONTINUE
   28 SNTHE = SIN(THETA)
      CSTHE = COS(THETA)
      DELK = DELTA *CSTHE/SNTHE
      DELJ = DELTA/SNTHE
      IFIVE = 5
    5 CONTINUE
      IFILM = 1
      I = 1
 4003 READ(OUTTP,4) RECX(I),(OD(J,I),J=1,I3)
CC
CC   CALCULATES EVERY FIFTH RECORD
      IF (IFIVE .GE. 5)  GO TO 4002
      IFIVE = IFIVE + 1
      GO TO 4003
 4002 IFIVE = 1
      DO 61 JJ = 1,I113
      KALC = 2*I113 -2 *(JJ-1)
      LOD(KALC,I) = LOD(I113 -(JJ-1),I)
   61 LOD(KALC-1,I) = .FALSE.
      DO 111  JJ=1,I113
      OD(JJ,I) = OD(JJ,I) *99/256
  111 CONTINUE
      WRITE (6,4001) RECX(I)
 4001 FORMAT('1 RECORD',I5,' - VALUES ARE 1-100, INVERSE INTENSITY'/)
      WRITE (6,401)  (OD(JJ,I), JJ=1,I113)
      II = 0
CC   READ READINGS > OR = 92 OF TAPE EDGING ON FILMS
 1150 II=II+1
      IF (I113-II) 1800,1800,1152
 1152 IF (LK -OD(II,I)) 1150,1150,1151
CCC
CCC DATA BEGINS IF > 8 READINGS  LESS THAN 92
 1151 IBEG(IFILM) = II
      II = II + 1
      K = 0
 1173 IF (LK - OD(II,I))  1150,1150,1174
 1174 II=II+1
      K = K + 1
      IF (3 - K) 1175,1175,1173
CCC ,DATA
 1161 II=II+1
 1175 IF (LK -OD(II,I)) 1162,1162,1161
CCC
CCC FILM ENDS IF >6 READINGS >92
 1162 II=II+1
      J = 0
      IF (LK - OD(II,I)) 1163,1163,1161
```

```
 1163 II=II+1
      J = J + 1
      IF (3-J) 1164,1164,1165
 1165 IF (LK -OD(II,I)) 1163,1163,1161
 1164 IEND(IFILM) = II-J-2
      IOUT = 2
      WRITE (6,401) IOUT,IBEG(IFILM),IEND(IFILM)
CCC GO DO NEXT FILM
      IFILM = IFILM + 1
      IF (IFILM-NFILM) 1150,1150,2000
C
C
C
CCC
CCC      THIS ONLY TAKES CARE OF NFILM = 2
CCC
 2000 IF (RECX(I) .GT. I1)  GO TO 2072
      IBGA = IBEG(IFILM-1) +IOFST(IFILM-1)   +2
      IBGAA = IBGA
      INDA = IEND(IFILM-1)   -2
      IBGB = IBEG(1)  +2
      INDB = IEND(1)   -2
      NMBA = INDA-IBGA+1
      NMBB = INDB-IBGB+1
      NMBC = NMBB * CSTHE
      NBPL = NMBB + 1
      NCPL = NMBC + 1
      AINCR = 1./CSTHE
      INS = D *SNTHE /DELTA
      INCS = INS /CSTHE
      IOUT = 3
      WRITE (6,401) IOUT,IBGA,INDA,IBGB,INDB,NMBA,NMBB,NMBC
  401 FORMAT (24I5)
 2072 CONTINUE
C     IBGA = IBGAA - 1
      DO 2055  IOFSET = 5,5
      IBGA = IBGAA- IOFSET   -1
      WRITE (6,3)   IBGA, IBGA, IBGA
      DO 2101  J=1,NMBB
      JOD = OD(IBGB+J-1,I)
      ORB(J) = 100 - JOD
C     ORB(J) = JOD
 2101 CONTINUE
      DO 2102 J=1,NMBC
      JOD = OD(IBGA+J-1,I)
C     ORC(J) = JOD
      ORC(J) = 100 - JOD
 2102 CONTINUE
      IOUT = 10
  444 FORMAT (4I5 ,(10E10.2))
  402 FORMAT (I4,(11E10.2))
  403 FORMAT (I4, (14F8.2))
CCC
CCC FIND ALPHA FOR FIRST APPROX
      DO 2001  KKK = 1,NMBC
      IF (KKK .GT. 1) GO TO 2003
 2002 KL = 1
      KU = INCS
      GO TO 2004
 2003 KL = KL + AINCR
      KU = KU + AINCR
      IF (KU .LE. NMBC)  GO TO 2004
      DO 3001 NM = NCPL,KU
```

```
 3001 ORC(NM) = 0.0
 2004 SUM = 0.
      DO 2005  J=KL,KU
 2005 SUM = SUM + ORC(J)
      ALPH(KKK) = 1. /(SUM *DELJ)
 2006 CCNTINUE
 2001 CONTINUE
CCC
CCC FIND FIRST APPR TO DENSITY RHO
      DO 2009  JJJ = 1,NMBC
      TEMP = ALPH(JJJ) *ORC(JJJ)
      DO 2010 J = 1,NMBB
      RHO(J,JJJ) = TEMP *ORB(J)
 2010 CCNTINUE
 2009 CCNTINUE
CCC
CCC ITERATE RHO UNIIL CONVERGENCE
CCC
      KITER = 1
CCC SEE IF B-PROJ IS SATISFIED
 2030 CNVB = 0.
      IF (KITER .LT. 10)  GO TO 3010
      WRITE (6,3011) RECX(I)
 3011 FORMAT (//'0 NO OUTPUT FOR RECORD',I5,'  DUE TO NO CONVERGENCE'/)
      GO TO 2038
 3010 KITER = KITER + 1
      DO 2011 J=1,NMBB
      SUM = 0.
      JMN = INCS + 1
      KU = 1. +(J-1)*CSTHE
      KL = KU - INS
      IF (KU .LE. NMBC) GO TO 3002
      DO 3003  NM=NCPL,KU
 3003 RHO(J,NM) = 0.0
 3002 IF (J .LE. JMN) KL=1
CCC
CCC SUM IS APPR TO B/PROJ
      DO 2012  M = KL,KU
 2012 SUM = SUM + RHO(J,M)
CCC
CCC ALPH IS RATIO OF B READING TO APPR
      SUM = SUM *DELK
      ALPH(J) = ORB(J) /SUM
 2011 CNVB = CNVB + ORB(J) - SUM
      CNVB = ABS(CNVB)
CCC
CCC MODIFY DENSITIES BY RATIO
      DO 2015  M = 1,NMBC
      DO 2016 J=1,NMBB
 2016 RHO(J,M)=ALPH(J)*RHO(J,M)
 2015 CONTINUE
      IOUT = 6
      WRITE (6,403)  KL,(ALPH(MM), MM=1,NMBB,5)
CCC
CCC SEE IF A-PROJ SATISFIED
      CNVA = 0.
      DO 2020  M=1,NMBC
      SUM = 0.
      JL = 1. +(M-1) /CSTHE
      JU = JL + INCS
C
CCC SUM IS APPR TO A-PROJ
```

```
       IF (JU .LE. NMBB) GO TO 2027
       DO 3004 NM=NBPL,JU
 3004 RHO(NM,M) = 0.0
 2027 DO 2021 J=JL,JU
 2021 SUM = SUM + RHO(J,M)
       SUM = SUM * DELJ
CCC ALPH IS RATIO
 2026 ALPH(M) = ORC(M) / SUM
 2020 CNVA = CNVA + ORC(M) - SUM
       CNVA = ABS (CNVA)
CCC
CCC MODIFY DENSITIES
       DO 2025 J=1,NMBB
       DO 2025 M = 1,NMBC
 2024 RHO(J,M) = ALPH(M)*RHO(J,M)
 2025 CONTINUE
       IOUT = 7
       WRITE (6,403)   JL,(ALPH(MM), MM=1,NMBC,5)
C
CCC TEST FOR CONVERGENCE, ITERATE
       IF (EPS*NMBB -CNVB) 2030,2031,2031
 2031 IF (EPS*NMBC -CNVA) 2030,2032,2032
C
CCC OUTPUT
CCC
CCC THIS WRITE FOR 2 FILMS ONLY
 2032 WRITE (6,415) RECX(I), IBGB,INDB,IBGA,INDA
  415 FORMAT (/////'O   OUTPUT FOR RECORD',I5,'  USING READINGS',I4,
      1' TO',I4,'  AND',I4,'  TO',I4,' , POSITIVE INTENSITIES'// 30X,
      2 'VIEW B SLICE OUTPUT'//)
       DO 2040  J=1,NMBB
       KU = 1. + (J-1) *CSTHE
       KL = KU - INS
       IF (J .LE. JMN) KL = 1
       DO 2033  KKC =KL,KU
       KOUT = KKC-KL+1
       IJK = IFIX(RHO(J,KKC) + .5)
       IF (IJK .GT. 12)  IJK = 12
       AOUT(KOUT) =ANB(2*IJK+1)
       ATWO(KOUT) =ANB(2*IJK+2)
 2033 CONTINUE
       JKN = KU-KL+2
       DO 2070 KOUT=JKN,15
 2070 ATWO(KOUT) =ANB(1)
       NOUT = JKN-1
       WRITE(6,414) J,(AOUT(KKC),KKC=1,NOUT)
  414 FORMAT (I4,5X,15(1X,A1))
       WRITE (6,2035)   (ATWO(KKC), KKC=1,15),J,(RHO(J,KC),KC=KL,KU)
 2035 FORMAT ('+',8X,15(1X,A1),10X,I4,3X,15F3.0)
C      WRITE (6,404) J, (RHO(J,KC), KC =KL,KU)
  404 FORMAT (//(30I4))
 2040 CONTINUE
       WRITE (6,2054)
 2054 FORMAT (////30X,'VIEW A SLICE OUTPUT'//)
       DO 2050  K=1,NMBC
       JL = 1. +(K-1)/CSTHE
       JU = JL + INCS
       DO 2051  JJC =JL,JU
       JOUT = JJC -JL +1
       IJK = IFIX(RHO(JJC,K) + .5)
       IF  (IJK .GT. 12)  IJK=12
       AOUT (JOUT) = ANB(2*IJK+1)
```

```
       ATWO(JOUT) = ANB(2*IJK+2)
 2051  CONTINUE
       JJN=JU-JL+2
       MOUT = JJN-1
       DO 2052  JOUT=JJN,15
 2052  ATWO(JOUT) = ANB(1)
       WRITE (6,414) K,(AOUT(JJC),JJC=1,MOUT)
       WRITE (6,2035) (ATWO(JJC),JJC=1,15),K,(RHO(JC,K),JC=JL,JU)
 2050  CONTINUE
       GO TO 2041
 1800  WRITE (6,405)
  405  FORMAT (///' ERROR'//)
 2041  CONTINUE
 2055  CONTINUE
 2038  IF (RECX(I) .LE. I2)  GO TO 5
       WRITE (6,991)
       WRITE (6,992)
  991  FORMAT ('1 A8MBB XXB 8E++*+==')
  992  FORMAT ('+ WMNMWO8IIW=*888-')
       END
```

Index

Index

About the Author

Sheldon S. Sandler is an associate professor of electrical engineering at Northeastern University, a research scientist in the Division of Engineering and Applied Physics at Harvard University, and a consultant to the Solar X-Ray Astronomy Group of American Science and Engineering. He has served as a consultant to several other corporations and universities; as a research associate in the Department of Physics of Horizon's Inc. in Cleveland, Ohio; as a staff member of the Antenna Group of the M.I.T. Lincoln Laboratory in Lexington, Massachusetts; and as a staff member of Electronic Communications, Inc., in Timonium, Maryland. From 1964 to 1965, Professor Sandler was a guest professor in the Institut für Hochfrequenztechnik at the Eidgenössische Technische Hochschule in Zürich, and in 1969/70 he was on sabbatical at the MRC Laboratory for Molecular Biology in Cambridge, England. He is the author of numerous original papers in technical journals and is the coauthor (with R.W.P. King and R.B. Mack) of *Arrays of Cylindrical Dipoles* (Cambridge University Press, 1968). Professor Sandler's present area of research is bioengineering; under a grant from the National Science Foundation, he is investigating the effect of electromagnetic waves on biological tissue. He received the B.S. in electrical engineering from Case Institute of Technology in 1954, the M.Eng. in electrical engineering from Yale University in 1955, the M.A. in applied physics from Harvard University in 1958, and the Ph.D. in applied physics from Harvard University in 1962. Professor Sandler is a member of Comm. VI of the International Scientific Radio Union and Sigma Xi.